STRATEGIC PREPARATION

STRATEGIC PREPARATION

TONY JEARY
THE RESULTS GUY™

RESULTS
FASTER!

PUBLISHING

Published by Results Faster Publishing in association with Clovercroft Publishing, Franklin, Tennessee

Cover Design by Debbie Manning Sheppard

Interior Design by Suzanne Lawing

Printed in the United States of America

978-1-948484-88-6

By failing to prepare, you are preparing to fail.
—BENJAMIN FRANKLIN

*I'm convinced after working with many of the world's
best for decades that "preparation" stands as its own
category in supporting success.*
—TONY JEARY

*Give me six hours to chop down a tree, and I will
spend the first four sharpening the axe.*
—ABRAHAM LINCOLN

Dedication and Honor

This is a special subject to me. All my life, preparation has been ingrained into my thinking and habits—mainly by observing, modeling, and then, later, by studying. I have committed my life to taking all that I've learned over the years and sharing that knowledge with others—including my kids, and, of course, my students and clients. I want to dedicate this work to both my father and my father-in-law, each of whom had a tremendous impact on my life and taught me the importance of daily preparation.

Growing up, my dad showed me how to be prepared for anything that may happen in life. From something as simple as buying extra supplies like a back-up lawn mower blade to investing in my vehicles for a higher resale value, he showed me how to look into the future and plan ahead.

Before my wife Tammy and I were married, I observed that my father-in-law had many of the same great qualities of my father, especially in regard to preparing his daughter to be successful in life. Even doing little things (that matter a lot) like ensuring his girls always had a new battery in their car or plenty of tread on their tires.

These patterns so impressed upon my mind that preparing—to save time, to reduce stress, to increase safety, to avoid hassle, to be ready for any challenge or opportunity—was the surest path to success.

Get ready (prepare) to expand your thinking, transforming these concepts from ideas to habits to a way of life.

We love helping winners win more. I'm so thankful for my two fathers, who shaped my thinking and my life, and I truly hope this book does the same for you!

Strategic preparation pays.

INTRODUCTION

How well do you prepare? Do you think there is another level for you? If so, please read on.

About three years ago SUCCESS magazine commissioned me in a joint venture to create an online video course called *RESULTS Faster!* that pulled together my first forty-four books. (We're privileged to be at fifty-seven now, and counting). We were fortunate to have Pam Henderson join us in that joint venture, who had been helping Tony Robbins develop his IP for almost two decades, and she helped us put together a really powerful course (a must watch at www.tonyjeary.com/resultsfaster).

As the course came together, we ended up with seven modules, each with three lessons, for a total of twenty-one lessons. It was so well received that we decided to do a whole book around it of the same title, *RESULTS Faster!* We soon realized that each one of those twenty-one lessons deserved to be a book, in and of itself, and so far we've written several. For example, we turned the powerful lesson on *High Leverage Activities* into a book we called *Leverage.* The book you have here is based on the lesson on preparation—hence the title, *Strategic Preparation*—which we've enhanced, organized, and published with substantial detail for you.

We're convinced that most people don't prepare to the level they could, so they don't often end up with the results they'd like to have. We believe preparation is a giant overlooked factor in achieving success and getting better and faster results.

Preparation pays! It involves thinking, which is one of the powerful secrets we share with our clients so they get much more favorable results. One particularly critical aspect of thinking we teach to our clients is preparing for the future with a balance of "doing it now" (including *Production Before Perfection*—see No. 25) and the discipline of delayed gratification (see No. 24). Delayed gratification is such an effective concept because it encompasses so many angles—such as long-term thinking, putting in effort up front, doing *Favors in Advance* (see No. 41), and nourishing relationships—that yield amazing results down the line. It's certainly a win to live in the present, and I do. Yet this book is about winning, winning more, and winning bigger in the future. That's why you'll want to not just read it; you'll want to study it and put it in the hands of every team member and every young person in your life.

We utilize stories and personal examples in the book to help raise your awareness and support the impact. Today I'm blessed to be able to strategize and advise many of the world's best because of my brand, my track record, and my sincere desire to help our clients win more and lose less. And that's probably come about because of the valuable decision I made years ago to prepare more than most.

Now, in hopes of you to read the whole book, let me highlight for you just a few of the ways I've prepared over the years, both professionally and personally. You may want to adopt many of these ideas, as well.

- Landscaping: We planted shrubs that were a foot tall; today our estate is surrounded by a beautiful wall of nature.

- Kids' marriages: When my daughters were three and six, my wife and I helped them list the twelve qualities of the men they would one day attract and marry. It worked! We have two great men added to our family with qualities tied to the list. Both of them are blessed to come from extraordinary families!

- Kids' resumes: We started our kids' resumes when they each turned eleven, and over the years we helped them grow it to one that is loaded with value and track record.

- Praying for grandkids: Within minutes of when my first son-in-law asked me if he could marry our daughter, I asked him to begin praying for his grandkids. When he asked why, I simply shared that we are a generational family. (Read my book *Family Wealth*.)

- Saving for college: I became a millionaire at the age of twenty-one, and yet because of market changes I was broke by the age of twenty-six. In spite of that, from the day our daughters were born, we started saving $150 a month for each one, just in case we needed it for their college tuition.

- Books: This is my fifty-eighth title. We publish, film, and document tons of works because we want to be ready to impact lives.

(Books can go where you can't go and can stay longer than you can stay.)

- Arsenal: Over thirty years ago TJI began building a best-practice library (for CRM, tradeshows, branding, marketing, merchandising, gifting, etc.) that today supercharges people's lives and helps them grow their business endeavors—hence my business theme, RESULTS Faster!

- Relationships: (Read my book *Rich Relationships, Rich Life.*) My electronic Rolodex consists of tens of thousands of contacts that we've been collecting and nourishing with *Favors in Advance* (FIA) for over forty years.

- Moving to our home: We built an estate that became a true home (we invested four years in planning it), where we were able to keep our kids in the same school for fifteen years. We prayed that God would use the property to impact lives—and He has!

- *Life Team*: I've attracted and nourished an exceptional *Life Team* for over thirty-five years such as Buz, my attorney for thirty-plus years; Mark, my coach for almost thirty-five years; Boden, my CPA for nearly thirty years; Nonie, my wonderful writer for right at two decades; and Tawnya and Eloise, my incredible business colleagues who have watched over my business affairs for almost two decades, as well.

- Learning: I've been studying results and success for an average of an hour a day since 1986 in order to gain insights and wisdom to pour into other people's future success.

- Marriage: Tammy and I have been together for over thirty years. She's special! The right spouse is a true gift. Prepare carefully!

A few years ago I coauthored a book entitled *Business Ground Rules* with my great friend and entrepreneur extraordinaire Peter Thomas. As a serial entrepreneur who has developed billions of dollars in real estate projects—from shopping centers to apartments and condominiums, to golf courses all across America and Canada—Peter contributed many excellent ideas to that book. Several of them are powerful preparation concepts that we've included in this book, as well, because we believe they will help take you to the next level as you prepare to achieve better results.

We believe if you really take to heart each one of these 100 ideas and chuck them up to the highest level, you'll have a real win from the time you invest in this book. You may already be doing some of these things; others you may have never thought of, and there may be others that you're doing in part but may be a little lax on. I sincerely hope this book impacts your life by impacting your thinking.

We've divided the 100 preparation ideas into thirteen categories:

1. Clarity

2. Focus

3. Execution

4. Time Mindset

5. Thinking

6. Relationships

7. Communication

8. Being Ready

9. Investing for your Future

10. Health

11. Arsenal

12. Force Multipliers

13. Habits

If by chance there's a particular category that interests you more than others, feel free to bounce around. The book is designed to have flexibility in a way that's very reader friendly. When I author books, I don't think about designing them the way I want them to be. Rather, I think about how the reader can best absorb the material their way, based upon what's most important to them. For example, most of my books (not this one, because of its unique design) have VIP's (very important points) at the end of each chapter, and the reader may want to just read those to quickly extract the meat of the book.

So how well do you prepare? Before you dive in, take a minute to rate your current preparation level below on a scale of 1 to 10 in each of the thirteen areas. (You may want to take a look at the table of contents to view the topics in each area before you rate yourself.)

	Category	Description	Rating
1.	Clarity	Start with clarity about your vision, goals, values, purpose, and standards; create a written plan and MOLO your life often.	
2.	Focus	Sharpen and maintain your focus; eliminate distractions; focus on results vs. activities.	
3.	Execution	Be intentional: Dwell on solutions, communicate your vision, measure everything, execute with speed, and use powerful self-talk.	
4.	Time Mindset	Manage your time by saying "no" often, creating *Elegant Solutions*, and prioritizing hourly; have a "do-it-now" attitude.	
5.	Thinking	Value daily thinking time; get a great coach and mentors to help you discover your *Blind Spots*; and understand you become what you think about.	
6.	Relationships	Rich relationships = rich life. Surround yourself with a powerful *Life Team* and positive, successful people; nourish your relationships; do *Favors in Advance*.	
7.	Communication	Have great meetings with clear objectives, clear preparation, and an aligned agenda; be ready for the tough questions; and become proficient in the strategic asset of *Presentation Mastery*™	
8.	Being Ready	Have a mindset that says, *I will always prep and be ready ahead of time;* be consistently organized; have backup for everything; plan for what-ifs; be presentation ready; and know your risk factor.	
9.	Investing for Your Future	Get advice that will help you uncover your *Blind Spots*. Strategically build your personal brand and develop a memorable, influential persona; plant seeds, invest in your future, and reward yourself often.	

10.	Health	Get clear on who you want to become, get good professional advice, and then build your health goals and actions around that vision. Control your diet, get the right exercises, and manage stress.	
11.	Arsenal	Keep an arsenal of tools to give you leverage in presenting your message, executing faster, and adding value. Exceed expectations by planning your arsenal ahead.	
12.	Force Multipliers	Utilize your phone to create leverage and multiply your results. Use Dropbox or an online system to back up your files. Take strategic notes and use checklists to maximize results.	
13.	Habits	Notice patterns and turn them into the right habits. Think like successful people think and do what successful people do. Execute to the point of habit, and strategically move things into the automatic zone. Strategically create foundational habits.	

How did you do? Do you do a great job in preparing in most of the categories, which puts you at about an 8 or a 9, or are you somewhere in the middle—perhaps a 4 or 5—on many of them and you know you need to do better? Or maybe you're way down on the chart in some of the categories and you're saying, *"That's definitely something I need to work on."* Wherever you are on that spectrum, this book can help you push that needle farther up the scale.

A key factor to my success, both personally and professionally, is that my parents and grandparents modeled preparation. Hence, I've prepared in so many ways for so many years, continually thinking about and weighing risk mitigation versus advancing the ball. That's what this book is all about.

I want to challenge you to mentally own preparation as a differentiator. In any situation, there is always someone who's the most prepared. Decide now that you're going to be that person, and make it part of your brand. A mindset that says, *I will always prepare and be ready ahead of time* is simply a philosophy that sparks success.

If this book resonates with you, I really hope you read my other books. For now, let's dig in to this one!

TABLE OF CONTENTS

I. CLARITY **19**
1. Get Clarity on What You Really Want. 21
2. Ensure You Are Clear on Your Values. 24
3. Craft a Purpose Statement 26
4. Know What Really Makes You Happy. 27
5. Set Goals for What You Want to Have, Share,
    Experience, Give, and Become. .30
6. Create a Written Plan for Virtually Everything 32
7. Future Pace 33
8. Document Potential Roadblocks .34
9. Get Clear on Your Risk Tolerance 36
10. Develop a Likeness Matrix 37
11. MOLO Your Life Often (More of, Less Of) 39
12. Live by Documented Standards,
    Both Personal and Professional .42

II. FOCUS **45**
13. Sharpen Your Focus Skill with More HLAs and Less LLAs 46
14. Focus on Results Versus Activity .49
15. Utilize the Power of Visualization 51
16. Maintain Your Personal Agenda in Hard Times 53

III. EXECUTION **55**
17. Live in Solutions. 56
18. Execute with Accountability. 58
19. Understand That Speed Matters. .60
20. Move to Mastery by Using Intentional Self-Talk. 61
21. Be Intentional About Everything. .64
22. Adhere to the 140-Percent Rule (Don't Overdo). 66
23. Channel Your Emotions and Control Your Ego. 67

IV. TIME MINDSET **69**
24. The More Time You Save, the More You
    Have to Invest Elsewhere 70

25. Practice Delayed Gratification as a
Master Principle of Winning 71
26. Have a "Do-It-Now" Mindset. 73
27. Say "No" Strategically (and Still Give
People What They Want) 75
28. Create Elegant Solutions 77
29. Appreciate and Invest Time in What You Want More Of. 80
30. Prioritize Hourly 82

V. THINKING. 83
31. You Become What You Think About .84
32. Find Great Mentors or Coaches. 86
33. Use Planned Spontaneity 88
34. Develop Sensory Acuity 90
35. Prepare with State Management 91
36. Wake up Early and Visualize Your Day. 92
37. Value Daily Thinking Time. 94
38. Avoid Fear, Uncertainty, and Doubt .95

VI. RELATIONSHIPS 97
39. Build a Powerful Life Team. 98
40. Establish an Informal Board of Advisors 99
41. Do Favors in Advance (FIA) 101
42. Surround Yourself with People More
Successful Than Yourself. 102
43. Build Your Own Brand by Helping Others Win 103
44. Express Gratitude. 105
45. Give Back. 107
46. Be Real. 108
47. Be a "Connector" 109
48. Be a Person of Influence 111
49. Focus on Your People of Influence 112
50. Understand and Utilize Personality Profiling 113
51. Hire Successful, Positive People. 115
52. Build Rich Relationships So You'll Have a Rich Life. 116
53. Listen Up! 119
54. Make Others Feel Significant 121
55. Provide Joy and Entertainment 122

VII. COMMUNICATION. **123**
56. Have Great Meetings 124
57. Rehearsing Helps Take You from the
    Unknown to the Known 126
58. Be Ready for Tough Questions. 127
59. Plan Cascading. 129
60. Study Presentation Mastery™ As a Strategic Asset. 130
61. Ask Questions to Get Leverage 132

VIII. BEING READY. **135**
62. Confidence Comes from Being Ready 136
63. Organize Every Day. 137
64. Have Backup for Everything. 138
65. Plan for What-ifs in Your Meetings. 139
66. Be Dependent on God. 140
67. Establish Rules Before You Start the Game 141
68. Benchmark for Best Practices. 142
69. Be "Presentation Ready" 143
70. Develop Perseverance 144

IX. INVESTING FOR YOUR FUTURE **145**
71. Uncover Your Blind Spots. *146*
72. Ensure a Powerful Personal Brand in the Future. 148
73. Develop a Memorable, Influential Persona 150
74. Work on Your Body Language and Appearance 152
75. Constantly Plant Seeds for Your Future Success 154
76. Invest in Yourself 155
77. Dig for Opportunities 156
78. Reward Yourself Often 158
79. Manage Your Energy, Not Just Your Time 159

X. HEALTH. **161**
80. Prepare to Live Healthy. 162
81. Prevent Disease by Controlling Your Diet 164
82. Prepare for Quality of Life with the Right Exercise. 166
83. Manage Stress by Being Clear Ahead on
    What Matters and Where You Are. 168
84. A Healthy Life Includes What You Think About,
    Let Go of, and Refuse to Believe 169

85. Remove Toxins to Stay Healthy 170
86. Make the Best Use of Supplements 172

X. ARSENAL **173**
87. The Bigger Your Arsenal the More Leverage You Have 174
88. Focus on Creating Extra Value by Building
    a Strong Arsenal /Tool Chest in Advance 176
89. You Have Less Stress with a More Solvable Tool Chest 177
90. Build a List of Fun, Valuable Public Domain URLs 178
91. Include a Picture of Your Family's
    Goals Wall in Your Arsenal 179

XII. FORCE MULTIPLIERS **181**
92. Your Phone Is a Huge Force Multiplier 182
93. Use Dropbox or an Online System 185
94. Take Strategic Notes 186

XIII. HABITS **187**
96. Notice Patterns and Turn Them into the Right Habits 188
97. Think Like Successful People Think and
    Do What Successful People Do 190
98. Prepare to Live at the Highest Level
    by Executing to the Point of Habit 192
99. Be Strategic About Moving Things
    into the Automatic Zone 193
100. Create Foundational Habits 195

Conclusion 198

I. CLARITY

*Go as far as you can see in this fast-paced world,
and then you can see farther.*
—Tony Jeary

1.
GET CLARITY ON WHAT YOU REALLY WANT

"Clarity" is one of the three foundational words that make up my *Strategic Acceleration* methodology: Clarity, Focus, and Execution. These three pillars of high achievers are the necessary tools for bringing you the results and success you want—faster. The most successful people design their own lives and then live their lives on purpose, and the first step is clarity.

Clarity is about understanding and documenting your targets clearly and determining the "why" behind reaching them (personally and professionally). It's about developing a clear vision, outlining priorities and objectives, and tackling goals with a real sense of urgency and focus.

There's a real pulling power that comes from investing ahead in getting clear about what you truly want. Clarity opens up new opportunities and connections and empowers you to make better strategic choices. In other words, gaining clarity is investing now for more and bigger wins down the road.

THERE'S A REAL PULLING POWER THAT COMES FROM INVESTING AHEAD IN GETTING CLEAR ABOUT WHAT YOU TRULY WANT.

Sometimes you may think you have clarity when, in reality, you haven't put much thought into it at all. You haven't asked yourself, *What do I truly want and why do I want it?* Being clear at the outset will have a huge impact as you work to reach your goals and realize your vision.

There's actually a scientific reason for that. Gaining clarity allows you to strategically take advantage of your reticular activating system (RAS), which is a set of nerves at the bottom of your brain that allows you to bring things into your brain that you need, want, or desire. When you have clarity about what you want, your brain allows relevant things to come into your brain.

Here's how that works: Have you ever bought a new vehicle and then, after a week or so, you look around and start seeing those same vehicles everywhere? And yet a few weeks before you bought the vehicle, you probably never even saw those vehicles on the road all around you. Why? It's because you had not told your brain (your RAS—your gatekeeper) to be interested; therefore, your brain did not even really detect seeing those cars at that point.

Here's another example. Let's say you're in the process of building your home, and you've been thinking about putting a chandelier in your dining room. So when you look up and see a chandelier in the room you're standing in, all of a sudden you're very interested and you look at all its distinctions. If you weren't building a house, you probably wouldn't be thinking about chandeliers; that chandelier would still be there, and yet your RAS wouldn't even care about it. Your brain likely wouldn't have even let it in, and you would not have even noticed what kind of light was in the room.

Since the reticular activating system allows things to come into your brain that you're interested in, gaining clarity about what you want is what triggers the law of attraction that allows what you care about to come in through your RAS. That has a huge impact on helping you achieve the goals you've set to get you where you want to go. You not only see the goals in your mind; you also begin to see things around you that will help you achieve your goals. If you don't have clarity about their importance, your RAS filters out things you might need to help you achieve your goals. If you really want to leverage your RAS, do these three things:

1. Write down your goals

2. Visualize your goals

3. Employ congruent self-talk

Clarity of vision gives you the mental substance to persevere and overcome obstacles. If you're not clear about what you truly want, your belief in your effort will not be powerful or compelling enough to sustain your efforts. When you lack clarity, you will find yourself being pushed toward living in problems.

Without a clear vision, you're just travelling and rarely arriving. A

CLARITY OF VISION GIVES YOU THE MENTAL SUBSTANCE TO PERSEVERE AND OVERCOME OBSTACLES.

clear vision pulls and energizes you toward getting what you want. I suggest you go as far as you can see in this fast-paced world, and then you can see farther. When you get more clarity as the weeks, months, and even years go down, you can make any tweaks or changes that are needed.

2.
ENSURE YOU ARE CLEAR ON YOUR VALUES

Prepare for your whole life, including your career (or even better, your vocation), by taking time up front to define what you value. Then set your goals in alignment with your values so you are prepared for designing your own life with congruence. When you take action on those goals, you can and will make better decisions, and you will enjoy a more intentional and successful, focused life.

A giant mistake that many people make is jumping right into setting their goals and skipping over clarifying their values. There's no doubt that everyone needs to be clear on their action plan; and yet most people don't take the time to step back and say, *What is my life all about?*

Your action plan should include your values-based strategy if you want to win big for the long haul. It's critical to establish clarity about what matters to you, what matters to your spouse if you happen to be married, and what matters for your team if you have a team. You don't want to create results faster and then find out they're the wrong results!

> YOUR ACTION PLAN SHOULD INCLUDE YOUR VALUES-BASED STRATEGY IF YOU WANT TO WIN BIG FOR THE LONG HAUL. YOU DON'T WANT TO CREATE RESULTS FASTER AND THEN FIND OUT THEY'RE THE WRONG RESULTS!

Do you have that clarity about what your values are? When people book time with me in my studio, I often have them do what I call a "values tournament" to clarify what's most important to them, using a special deck of cards I've developed that contains sixty different values. We've listed those sixty values below, and we invite you to go through them and select your top twenty values by numbering them in the spaces to the side. Then select your top ten out of those twenty. That doesn't mean you don't value the other things; you're just choosing the ten that mean the most to you.

_____ Affection	_____ Friendship	_____ Personal Brand
_____ Alignment	_____ Fun	_____ Personal Improvement
_____ Altruism	_____ Generosity	_____ Personal Salvation
_____ Appearance	_____ Genuineness	_____ Philanthropy
_____ Appreciated	_____ Happiness	_____ Power
_____ Attitude	_____ Harmony	_____ Productivity
_____ Cleanliness	_____ Health	_____ Recognition
_____ Congruence	_____ Honesty	_____ Respect
_____ Contentment	_____ Humility	_____ Results
_____ Cooperation	_____ Inner Peace	_____ Romance
_____ Creativity	_____ Inspiration	_____ Routine
_____ Education	_____ Intimacy	_____ Security
_____ Effectiveness	_____ Joy	_____ See the World
_____ Efficiency	_____ Knowledge	_____ Simplicity
_____ Fairness	_____ Lifestyle	_____ Solitude
_____ Faith	_____ Loved	_____ Spiritual Maturity
_____ Fame	_____ Loyalty	_____ Status
_____ Family	_____ Motivation	_____ Wealth
_____ Financial Security	_____ Openness	_____ Winning
_____ Freedom	_____ Organization	_____ Wisdom

If you want congruency in every area of your life, you must start by having clarity about what you truly value.

3.
CRAFT A PURPOSE STATEMENT

A deeper level of life preparation is to carefully think about and craft a purpose statement. Once you define your values, it's easier (notice I said easier—not easy) to write a single sentence or two that encapsulates your life's purpose. If you're living on purpose, you're living in the zone.

IF YOU'RE LIVING ON PURPOSE, YOU'RE LIVING IN THE ZONE.

Let me share with you my purpose statement:

The purpose of my life is to live each day happy and with the Lord, turning people toward God through my words and works, always being a great father, husband, and friend, while giving, improving, and serving all people.

Why do you do what you do? It's very important to get very clear on your purpose as you prepare for life. As you're making decisions every day, you'll want to live on purpose doing exactly what your purpose statement says.

4.
KNOW WHAT REALLY
MAKES YOU HAPPY

Most people value happiness, and yet how many think of preparing for life by choosing happiness (or, more specifically, joy)?

I have studied happiness for many years, and I've discovered that there are certain things that can greatly contribute to living a happy and joyful life. Happiness is a choice that people elect to bring into their lives despite their circumstances.

Both joy and happiness are positive emotions that are satisfying in nature, and yet many people don't realize the big difference between the two. *Happiness is an emotion and is temporary, mostly dependent upon outside circumstances; joy is an attitude of the heart.* You can be both joyful and happy at the same time; and yet, just because you're happy, it doesn't mean you're joyful.

Joy is an inner peace that is present despite your circumstances. Happiness is a feeling of pleasure or contentment that is externally triggered by a pleasant experience and/or environment, often based on other people, things, places, thoughts, and events. Joy is more consistent and is cultivated internally. It comes when you make peace with who you are and your purpose in life. You actually have control over

JOY IS AN INNER PEACE THAT IS PRESENT DESPITE YOUR CIRCUMSTANCES. HAPPINESS IS A FEELING OF PLEASURE OR CONTENTMENT THAT IS EXTERNALLY TRIGGERED BY A PLEASANT EXPERIENCE AND/OR ENVIRONMENT, OFTEN BASED ON OTHER PEOPLE, THINGS, PLACES, THOUGHTS, AND EVENTS. JOY IS MORE CONSISTENT AND IS CULTIVATED INTERNALLY. IT COMES WHEN YOU MAKE PEACE WITH WHO YOU ARE AND YOUR PURPOSE IN LIFE.

both joy and happiness in your life.

I believe there are five key areas of life that are critical to finding and living a life of happiness. These five areas create the acronym SMILE—Significance, Money, Inspiration, Lifestyle, and Engagement—and then we add another "S" at the end because all of them together equal Success. (See my book coauthored with my Australian friend Dr. Daryl Holmes called *Living Life Smiling*.) Using the simple *Happiness Index* below, rate your current level of happiness within each of the first five areas from 1 to 20 (with 20 being the highest). Then total your score to find your starting point.

HAPPINESS INDEX

(Rate where you are in each area from 1 to 20, with 20 being the highest.)

What	Description	Score
Significance **S**	*You do what matters most to you.* You have alignment of values, and you have clearly defined your purpose and live this purpose intentionally and fully. You have self-acceptance, you focus on your unique strengths, and you have a strong sense of inner peace.	
Money **M**	*You have cash flow, reserves, financial security, and financial freedom, and you do valuable things for others.* You have acquired wealth, are content with your circumstances, and have a satisfying net worth. You give back to others and have a sense of security.	
Inspiration **I**	*You have positive emotions and are energized. You have a high level of self-motivation.* You are generally an optimistic person and create experiences regularly that inspire you. You have a great sense of self-worth and enjoy the small things as well as the big things.	
Lifestyle **L**	*You put habits into place that support the lifestyle you want.* You are patient (yet persistent) in going after your goals. You place a high degree of importance on your health in the form of diet, exercise, and a positive mental mindset. You value creating a home versus having a house, and you genuinely enjoy the journey of your life.	
Engagement **E**	*You become immersed in your work, the people you love, your friendships, and your leisure.* You have great, balanced relationships. You surround yourself with positive people and eliminate toxic ones. You have a solid Life Team supporting you. You have a healthy respect for yourself, others, and authority.	
SUCCESS **S**	*You live a happy, fulfilled life with purpose and alignment, and ensure that others win!* You are excited about what you're doing, sticking to what matters during tough times, and living a life you can be proud of and that others will want to share with you.	TOTAL SCORE

5.
Set Goals for What You Want to Have, Share, Experience, Give, and Become

Most people set goals for their life on just on what they want to have (like a big house or a certain vehicle), and yet that's only one piece of the puzzle. Your goals should include not only what you want to have; they should also include what you want to share, what you want to experience, what you want to give, and, perhaps most importantly, what you want to become. Having clearly defined goals allows you to literally design your own life.

As we talked about in "Get Clarity" (No. 1), you attract what you define, visualize, and speak to yourself about. Use all three processes to support making yourself ready to accomplish your goals by opening the RAS gate to your mind.

For example, you might want to make a life list of your top 100 goals in order to prepare yourself to be more motivated and inspired about your future. I did that in 1986, when I first came across that great idea. (I love uncovering great ideas, and I hope you do, as well. In fact I've invested the largest part of my life studying and looking for best practices, models and nuances that help produce faster and better results. When I find them, I sort and organize them in order to share them with my clients. That's really what I do, and I'm so blessed to get to change lives and grow companies by doing so.) I was a young man, then, and I started listing 100 things I wanted to achieve in my life in preparation for where I was going. I couldn't quite get to 100 at the time,

> YOUR GOALS SHOULD INCLUDE NOT ONLY WHAT YOU WANT TO HAVE; THEY SHOULD ALSO INCLUDE WHAT YOU WANT TO SHARE, WHAT YOU WANT TO EXPERIENCE, WHAT YOU WANT TO GIVE, AND, PERHAPS MOST IMPORTANTLY, WHAT YOU WANT TO BECOME.

so I've added to it over the years. I've been careful to list things I not only wanted to have, but what I wanted to share, give, experience, and become, as well.

That list has driven me all these years, and as of today I've been able to put an "x" in the box of about eighty-five of them. One of the first things on my list was to have an incredible family, and that's exactly what I'm so blessed to have today. I also wanted to hang out with wise people and to gain the wisdom to be able to pour into others in a big way, and I'm happy to say there's an "x" in that box, too.

It's so powerful when you take the time to prepare and plan ahead and put really careful thought into your mind (which activates your RAS) about the 100 items you want to have, experience, share, give, and of course become.

Don't be a squatter—someone who gets a really great idea and then doesn't do squat about it. I wasn't a squatter. I did it and really prepared the basis for my goalsetting for the rest of my life. I encourage you to do the same.

6.
Create a Written Plan for Virtually Everything

Your progress, success, and accomplishments will be more thorough, accurate, and faster if you have a plan in place. It's that simple and that powerful. In the basic sense, a plan should have the goal/objective or outcomes desired for each item, as well as who does what by when, and how often. Create a written plan for virtually everything you do, and in most cases keep the plan handy and in your phone to access quickly.

7.
FUTURE PACE

"Future Pace" is an NLP (Neuro-Linguistic Programming) term (see my books on NLP), and it refers to preparing the minds of others to see the benefits of going where you may want them to go in the future. By speaking about what the future will (or could) hold, you can prepare them to partner with you on a project or a venture, to accomplish or experience something together, to utilize your product or service, etc. You can also use future pacing to allow yourself to see the benefits of the potential of winning from a future happening.

> BY SPEAKING ABOUT WHAT THE FUTURE WILL (OR COULD) HOLD, YOU CAN PREPARE PEOPLE TO PARTNER WITH YOU ON A PROJECT OR A VENTURE, TO ACCOMPLISH OR EXPERIENCE SOMETHING TOGETHER, TO UTILIZE YOUR PRODUCT OR SERVICE, ETC.

Future pacing makes it easier for you or the other person to take smaller steps leading up to your future vision. If they (or you) have already thought about the future idea becoming a reality, it's relatively easy for them to take the first steps and gain inertia toward your cause. This kind of mental preparation is used by many top performers. Since the body and mind form one system, it prepares and primes the body for the actual situation.

You can facilitate future pacing by communicating way beyond the first steps what you want to have happen. (Example: A mattress salesperson may say, "You're going to enjoy many wonderful nights of sleep on this mattress.") Expectations are self-fulfilling prophecies. Give the brain strong positive images of success so it's programmed to think in those terms and makes success more likely.

8.
DOCUMENT POTENTIAL ROADBLOCKS

Get clear on potential "stoppers," and make sure that, with the right preparation, they don't happen.

When you are preparing for any event, ask yourself, *What could possibly happen?* When you're making a presentation or leading an important meeting with a client, what could happen? What are the potential roadblocks? If you have a team, brainstorm with your team members about what could happen ahead, and resolve any roadblocks in advance. The more you prepare smartly, the more you make sure any obstacles or roadblocks don't get in your way.

We'll talk about *High Leverage Activities* (HLAs) in the next category ("Focus"). My favorite tool for helping people I coach get clear on their HLAs is the *Accelerator Matrix* we've included below. With this tool, once you identify your HLAs (focus areas) and your accelerators (primary actions), you can then determine and document what roadblocks you will need to prepare to go through, around, or over.

I encourage you to use this matrix, either for yourself or your organization, or both. It's a very simple yet powerful tool that will help you prepare for "what if's" associated with any of your HLAs—and thus maximize your results.

> WHEN YOU ARE PREPARING FOR ANY EVENT, ASK YOURSELF, WHAT COULD POSSIBLY HAPPEN? BRAINSTORM WITH YOUR TEAM MEMBERS ABOUT WHAT COULD HAPPEN AHEAD, AND RESOLVE ANY ROADBLOCKS IN ADVANCE.

ACCELERATOR MATRIX

Overall Objectives:			
#	HLAs / Focus Areas	Accelerators (Primary Actions)	Roadblocks to Bust
1.			
2.			
3.			
4.			
5.			
6.			
7.			
8.			

9.
Get Clear on Your Risk Tolerance

So many people are not clear on their risk tolerance, whether it involves investing, operating a business, or participating in adventurous activities. For example, when you're flying down the mountain on skis, you might look over and see people skiing next to trees and going over moguls. They're living in danger land. Well, that's not where I want to be. My risk tolerance is not that high. Yes, I like adventure; however, I enjoy doing too many other things in my life to take that big a risk of being injured.

In the book I coauthored with my great friend Peter Thomas, *Business Ground Rules*, Peter talks about the importance of not being afraid to dig deep for answers in order to asses risk in business deals. Know everything you need to know. The only dumb question is sometimes the question you don't ask. Always carry out a complete due diligence on the prospective deal—including on the people involved in the deal, the communication, the finances, and the timing. People think they're being courageous and bold by being risk takers. Contrary to popular belief, however, great entrepreneurs are not risk takers—they're risk assessors.

I think all the time about my risk tolerance in everything I do, and I would encourage you to do the same. Know your risk tolerance in all areas of your life. The more you think clearly and know your risk parameters, the easier it is to make fast and smarter decisions—on where you go, what you do, who you hang out with, how you approach new relationships, and what to say "no" to more easily.

10.
DEVELOP A LIKENESS MATRIX

This is a great idea to help you prepare for success in every area of your life. Create a Likeness Matrix that contains a list of things you want to model. (I've included my personal Likeness Matrix below to give you an example.) Just look around you to see the best of whatever you need or want to grow your effectiveness—whether it's in your business or in your personal life—put in it your Likeness Matrix, and then mirror part or all of it. What you like most you can either attract, buy, or build.

LIKENESS MATRIX

	Subject	Example	Distinctions	How
1.	Leverage TIME	Barrel Walk	Has people waiting in waiting room to slide in and see him next when he's ready	Processes and powerful team
2.	Office Team Support	Joel Katz	Valet service, details handled	Staff who gets it
3.	Environment	Ritz Carlton	Pristine, organized, clean	Home team and staff
4.	Grounds	Cesar's Palace	Manicured, flawless	Gardeners, lawn service
5.	Picnic Area	Japanese Hotel Garden	Serene, peaceful	Gardeners, lawn service
6.	Database	Kyle Wilson	Large, organized, systematic	Software and dedication
7.	Affiliate/Promoter Databank	Brian Tracy	Large, organized, systematic	Software and nourishment
8.	Reputation	Zig Ziglar	Esteemed, respected, Christian	Follow-through
9.	Accounting	Jerry Johnson	Daily critical success factors	Clarity and systems

10.	Brand	Ken Blanchard	Business guru	Breakthrough book, presentation arsenal, including web
11.	Business Legacy	Dale Carnegie	Life, presentations, evergreen	Continued focus on giving value
12.	Behind Scenes	Regal Shoes	Daily inspections of organized readiness	Checklists and discipline
13.	Pipeline Waiting List	President of US	Booked out by the minute	Reputation, marketing, systems
14.	Thinking	Robert Schuller	Possibilities	Right paradigms
15.	Rolodex	Ron Lusk	Power of calls to get things done	Systems, discipline, nourishment
16.	Thinning Mentality	Pi	No junk, minimalist	Thinking and discipline
17.	Personal Assistant	Zig's personal assistant	28-year history of thinking/doing what Zig would think and do	Training and thinking and discipline
18.	Business Manager	Jack Hayford's	Handling details surrounding	Synergistic thinking
19.	Respect	Giuliani	Track record, visible	Proven Results
20.	Readiness	Lou Achilles	Body was free of stuff	Thinking and practice

11.
MOLO YOUR LIFE OFTEN (MORE OF, LESS OF)

MOLO is a very powerful—and yet very simple—activity that can literally change your life. (Do a search on YouTube for "Peter Thomas Endorses Tony Jeary," and watch a powerful three-minute video.) It's basically preparing you for success by showing you which activities you should eliminate. First, you want to determine what you want more of and what you want less of, and then you need to determine what you need to do more of and what you need to do less of in order to get there.

> MAKING A LIST OF WHAT YOU WANT MORE OF AND LESS OF IS EXTREMELY IMPACTFUL IN MAXIMIZING YOUR TIME.

The goal of any audit is to help you create a better allocation of your time, effort, and resources so you can get greater returns and greater results. That's what a MOLO can do. It's an audit of your life that can show you where you're wasting your efforts, often in small ways. And it also can help you get clear on where you should be spending your time to get more "bang for your buck," so to speak, so you can significantly move the results needle.

Making a list of what you want more of and less of is extremely impactful in maximizing your time. You can do this not only for your personal life, but for your professional life, as well; in fact, you should do both.

I've included a sample MOLO matrix below that you can easily duplicate on a sheet of paper. However, if you're going to invest the time in doing a MOLO audit, make sure you're also going to take the action you say you're going to take. A MOLO audit is a fantastic focusing tool, and yet you have to execute—you have to do what you've written down.

MOLO (More Of...Less Of)		

What do we need to do more of?

#	What	Why	Who
1			
2			
3			
4			
5			

What do we need to do less of?

#	What	Why	Who
1			
2			
3			
4			
5			

What do we need to start doing?

#	What	Why	Who
1			
2			
3			
4			
5			

What do we need to stop doing?			
#	What	Why	Who
1			
2			
3			
4			
5			
What do we need to do differently?			
#	What	Why	Who
1			
2			
3			
4			
5			

When you start using the principle of MOLO to focus your efforts, it will increase your effectiveness immensely. It will also give you more time and energy to put toward those activities that provide the most leverage in your life and business.

12.
LIVE BY DOCUMENTED STANDARDS, BOTH PERSONAL AND PROFESSIONAL

One of the most effective distinctions, by far, that will prepare you to advance toward achieving the results you want in any area of your life is documenting and living by personal and business standards. Cultures are built around standards. Standards really do matter at the highest level. We all have them, although most people are not strategic enough to write them down. The benefits from doing so are endless.

> MANY OF THE BEST OPPORTUNITIES HAPPEN WHEN THE PEOPLE AT THE TOP HAVE THEIR STANDARDS DOCUMENTED.

As you know by now, I've work with some of the brightest people in the world—people who have run extremely successful enterprises of all different kinds. One thing I've found most interesting is that many of the best opportunities happen when the people at the top have their standards documented.

People at the top want the people in their organizations below them to know how they think. And that includes anyone who joins their team, whether it's large or small. For the most part, leaders at the top have experienced and figured out plenty of things, and they've developed personal systems and processes that work. Yet sometimes it takes weeks and months, or even years, for others in their organization to understand the flow, priorities, and expectations of the leader—*unless* they have documented standards and have taken the time to say, "If you're going to play on my team, here are the standards we live by."

The super performers actually make these written guidelines part of their culture. They've taken the time to document their standards, post them, and teach them, so when new people are on-boarded it's an easy matter of saying, "Here are our standards." Then a new team member can be prepared to align with the team's workflow must faster and easier. Showing them the standards right up front enables them to produce at a higher level, and everyone wins.

I'm convinced, however, that standards go way beyond just on-boarding someone effectively to your team. I believe they are a big part of advancing toward the mastery level. People at that level have standards for themselves, and they have standards for others that either deploy on their behalf, join their team, or both.

SUPER PERFORMERS ACTUALLY MAKE THEIR WRITTEN STANDARDS PART OF THEIR CULTURE.

I encourage you to take the time now to document both your personal standards and your professional standards. Personal standards set the stage for minimal distractions, guide your decisions, and help you say "no" more often so you can get rid of *Low-Leverage Activities*. I have twelve personal daily standards that help me live a life of mastery.

Your professional standards could be just for you and those you might delegate to, or they could be for those you recruit to your team or organization. They could be for your department, or they could be for a whole enterprise or even multiple companies in your holding company if you happen to be at that level. I have posters of my ten business standards (shown below) put up in every room in my office. I also have my team include them in the very first in-person interview when they're recruiting someone for our firm. In fact, that's one of our standards. They tell the person being interviewed that if we make them an offer, they need to know that these standards are solid expectations of how we operate, and they need to make sure they can live with them.

Performance Standards

*Our Mantra: Give Value; Do More Than Is Expected...*make every person, place, or thing you are a part of better.

1. **SAVE TONY'S TIME**, keeping him in front of and serving our clients.

2. **KAIZEN** means constant improvement for all team members... ongoing **COEs**, personal **SWOTs**, and **MOLO** refinements.

3. Keep everything clean and **ORGANIZED**... adds to our brand and makes us always ready.

4. Constant **LISTMAKING**... ensures prioritizing, accountability, and execution of faster results (including **CSFs**.)

5. Over-**COMMUNICATE** and calculate...helps ensure efforts are maximized. Avoid absolutes—words like "never," "always," and "can't"—because all things are possible.

6. **FOCUS**ed efforts on new flow of business/revenue. Daily priorities include pipeline management, SOW development, and processing receivables. Remember, cash is king!

7. Do Favors in Advance (**FIA**)—sharing, giving, and helping others win.

8. **DO THINGS NOW!** Operate with a mindset of quick action and speed to completion while using *Production Before Perfection*. Manage procrastination.

9. **PROACTIVE** in everything. (Think ahead, prep ahead, do ahead, invoice ahead, deliver ahead, and exceed expectations all around—internally and externally.)

10. **TEAM** approach—overlap, cross-support, encourage, and leverage each other's expertise; and together, keep all eyes on getting things done, completed and **RESULTS** produced hourly, daily, and weekly.

Get clear on and document your standards today. You'll be amazed at how powerful this one distinction can be toward preparing you for success in your life.

II. FOCUS

That's been one of my mantras—focus and simplicity.
Simple can be harder than complex: You have to work hard to get
your thinking clean to make it simple. But it's worth it in the end
because once you get there, you can move mountains.
—STEVE JOBS

Concentrate all your thoughts upon the work at hand.
The sun's rays do not burn until brought to a focus.
—ALEXANDER GRAHAM BELL

Focus will help you identify and concentrate on what
matters the most for the success of your vision, and it
will help you filter out distractions that hinder its progress.
—TONY JEARY

13.
SHARPEN YOUR FOCUS SKILL WITH MORE HLAS AND LESS LLAS

Focus is the opposite of distraction; it's a skill that most people need to learn. You can prepare for life better by sharpening this skill.

One way to do that is to understand and utilize the concept of *High Leverage Activities* (HLAs). No single skill or habit has a more powerful impact on results than the ability to eliminate distractions and focus on your *High Leverage Activities*. The clearer you are on your priorities, the better you are able to say "no" and do what matters most with your time and energy. Success is a results contest, and achieving superior results is based upon eliminating distractions that plague your daily time. You have to be able to spend your time on what matters most.

Leverage is the ability to influence something in a way that multiplies the outcome of the efforts without a corresponding increase in the consumption of resources. You can leverage your time, then, by doing your *High Leverage Activities* (HLAs) about 70 percent of your time.

Here's how that works: There are 168 hours in a week. We sleep for about 56 hours (8 hours a night), and we use roughly 12 hours for maintenance. That leaves about 100 hours to spend, and most people generally

> WE SHOULD THINK ABOUT AND IDENTIFY THOSE HLAS THAT WILL HAVE THE MOST IMPACT ON OUR RESULTS, BOTH PERSONALLY AND PROFESSIONALLY, AND FOCUS 70 PERCENT OF OUR TIME ON THOSE HLAS IN BOTH AREAS.

spend about 50 of those hours a week in their personal lives and about 50 in their professional lives. When we identify those HLAs that will have the most impact on our results and focus 70 percent of our time on those HLAs, both personally and professionally, we would be spending roughly 35 hours in each area on the pre-determined activities that will get us the best results.

Some examples of *High Leverage Activities* might be coaching and nourishing your team members, impacting those you serve, planning your day, and sharpening your skills. Defining your HLAs starts by knowing where you are and where you want to go. When you determine those two pieces of information, you'll see that there's a gap between them—and that gap should be filled with the HLAs you need to focus on in order to get you where you want to go.

Let me share with you my HLAs as examples, to help you better understand the concept.

These are my five personal HLAs:

1. Prayer

2. Spending time with my wife

3. Spending time with my family

4. Doing things that are health related, including walking, exercising, eating right, and even relaxing and counting my blessings

5. Loving people. I love to encourage and nourish the people around me. That could include writing a note to someone, sending an email, or making a phone call to my mom and loving on her.

So I should invest 70 percent of my 50 hours, or about 35 hours of my week, doing those things.

Now here are my five professional HLAs:

1. Attracting strong, qualified business.

2. Delivering great value. (Remember, my mantra is "Give value; do more than is expected.")

3. Clarifying the direction for my own operation.

4. Gaining wisdom. I'm in the wisdom business; so that means I need to constantly be sharpening my wisdom by studying, reading, and documenting my business acumen so I have a strong wisdom arsenal to share with people.

5. Nourishing my connections. I have a big rolodex, which means I have a large number of contacts I need to nourish. I do that in a variety of ways, including autographing books and sending them

(or other gifts) to people, as well as helpful websites, vendor lists, etc.

If something comes into my life that doesn't fit into one of those five categories, I have to weigh it very carefully before I say "yes" to it.

I encourage you to use the Accelerator Matrix we included in No. 8 ("Documenting Potential Roadblocks") to help you document both your personal and your professional HLAs.

14.
FOCUS ON RESULTS VERSUS ACTIVITY

People (in fact, the whole world) prize results, so focus ahead on what you want and what you should do to get the best results. We've talked about getting there by identifying and focusing on your *High Leverage Activities* (HLAs); however, you also need to think about things to avoid—*Low Leverage Activities* (LLAs)—to ensure you stay on track and focused.

Low Leverage Activities (LLAs) are those things that steal your time, such as wasted meeting time, doing activities that subordinates should be doing, spending time on prolonged telephone calls, and chasing down things you need because you are unorganized. They're activities that don't lead to the results you want. Most people burn fifteen to twenty hours a week in things they shouldn't be doing. If you want the best results, you have to get more organized and get rid of those LLAs.

> ACTIVITIES DON'T COUNT! RESULTS DO!

In general, what percentage of your time do you invest in *High Leverage Activities*, and what percentage of your time do you spend in *Low Leverage Activities*? Think about how much of your time you invest doing the things that truly matter the most, and then think of all of the activities you do that waste many of your minutes each day.

KEYS TO ELIMINATING DISTRACTIONS

Let me give you my four keys to eliminating distractions:

1. Make good daily lists.

2. Be organized to the max.

3. Schedule your time on your calendar! (In order to own your calendar, you have to learn to say "no" to certain things.)

4. Constantly audit yourself. At the end of the day you say, *How did I do? Was I actually productive and focus on results, or did I just do*

a ton of activities? Activities don't count! Results do!

Many people fill their day with activities on a to-do list and miss out on doing the most important. Know what matters and why, and then make sure you eliminate your LLAs.

15.
UTILIZE THE POWER OF VISUALIZATION

*Planning: Do all you can do to enhance the likelihood
of the outcome you envision becoming reality.*
—TONY JEARY

Remember the reticular activating system (RAS) we talked about in No. 1 ("Get Clarity on What You Really Want")? It's that set of nerves at the bottom of your brain that allows you to bring things into your brain that you need, want, or desire. Getting clarity about what you want so your brain will grant access to things that will help you achieve the goals is the first step. To help that process along, though, I suggest you use the power of visualization to keep your brain "motivated," if you will, to allow the right things in.

Remember, one of the keys to leveraging the RAS is visualizing your goals. Visualization is actually a very important piece of the puzzle. It's imperative that you keep your goals in front of you at all times, because visualization has a powerful effect on your transformation. It drives your desires and produces the voluntary change that will help you achieve results faster. Make sure, though, that what you're visualizing is congruent with what you write down, and then put your visualization pieces everywhere—in your bedroom, in your closet, on your phone, in your bathroom, and anywhere else you will see it every day. Use things like vision boards, posters, and pictures. Get your family involved, and create a personal/family/business goals wall.

KEEP YOUR GOALS IN FRONT OF YOU AT ALL TIMES, BECAUSE VISUALIZATION HAS A POWERFUL EFFECT ON YOUR TRANSFORMATION.

I personally believe vision boarding has more of an impact than anything else you can do, (as far as goal setting best practices) because it helps you mentally and emotionally link your vision to your goals and makes it come alive to you. My vision board has had such a dramatic impact on my family and my life that I want to encourage you to do the same thing—build a board that shows who you want to become, what you want to share, what you want to experience, and what you want to have.

I have a big vision board in my garage, so when I pull into my garage I can see my goals. Here's a picture of my current vision board:

I visualize everything, and I study my vision board every day. For most of my girls' lives, I visualized who they were going to marry. As a matter of fact, when they were three and six years old we got a wedding picture frame, and we put a picture of the two of them on the bride side. On the groom side we put a list of twelve characteristics of the guys they would eventually date and marry. Over the years, we talked about it and prayed about it, and they became the young ladies who would attract guys with those twelve characteristics. As of this publication date both my daughters have found two wonderful men who match that list. I even visualize my health goals. If you open my medicine cabinet, you'll see visualizations of the type of body I want to have. I look at it every day and it motivates me.

16.
MAINTAIN YOUR PERSONAL AGENDA IN HARD TIMES

Maintain your personal agenda in hard times, no matter what comes your way. By being clear in advance of what you value and then focusing on those values as you go, you increase your strength to make right decisions.

This was one of the topics Peter Thomas contributed to our book Business Ground Rules, and it's really a vital piece in preparing for your success. Some people forget this; and when they hit a roadblock or obstacle, it disrupts everything they had planned and impacts the way they think about themselves, their business, and others. You simply cannot cave when things go wrong. You have to maintain your personal agenda and stay the course.

Life is a series of peaks and valleys, and obstacles are inevitable. You must keep pushing through. When you're in turmoil, it's an excellent time to set some new personal objectives.

> YOU SIMPLY CANNOT CAVE WHEN THINGS GO WRONG. YOU HAVE TO MAINTAIN YOUR PERSONAL AGENDA AND STAY THE COURSE.

Build an environment that motivates you and will help you through those rough patches, and also realize that the world is not perfect. There are billions of people in it, and sometimes they can impact you negatively. The question is, how do you cope? How will you remain focused on your goals and relationships? One way is to deflect any drama, and minimize it when you can.

I remember a time when one of my employees called because her car broke down, as it had several times in the past. I had helped rescue her each time before, and it ate up valuable time. Because it seemed to be a pattern, I didn't engage in the drama or attempt to solve her problem this time; I simply encouraged her to solve it. My personal agenda on that particular day was to keep moving forward and create success, so I didn't let her problem or the fact that she may or may not show up ruin my day. I just kept my course.

Think about your personal agenda (your goals) for each day, and move toward it. If you take on everyone's problems, they become yours. They can negatively impact your mind and can be a huge drain on your energy and resources. There are always distractions that threaten the accomplishments you want to make.

Sometimes the problem is so big that you have to get involved. Just stay focused, stay on the path to clarity, and realize that life's not perfect. Maintain the clarity of your vision, and continually take action toward that vision. Use your support systems and rely on your *Life Team* to keep you focused. That's what they're there for.

Without a vision there is no solid foundation to tie your objectives (small steps to follow today) to your goal. Clarity of vision keeps your goals in perspective so they are always in the forefront of your mind as you execute, regardless of the obstacles that enter your day.

III. EXECUTION

Having a vision for what you want is not enough.
Vision without execution is hallucination.
—Thomas A. Edison

No excuses. No explanation. You don't win on emotion.
You win on execution.
—Tony Dungy

A good plan violently executed now is
better than a perfect plan tomorrow.
—George Patton

17.
LIVE IN SOLUTIONS

If you choose to live in solutions, the world eagerly awaits your dreams and provides every tool and opportunity you need to turn them into reality.
—TONY JEARY

The most successful people don't dwell on problems; they dwell on solutions. It's all about perspective. When you learn how to think strategically, you arrive at a whole new level of thinking that focuses on providing solutions to the problems that arise when change happens, often fast and without warning.

> THE MOST SUCCESSFUL PEOPLE DON'T DWELL ON PROBLEMS; THEY DWELL ON SOLUTIONS.

For example, salespeople may take a tactical approach to change by sharpening their cold-calling scripts. A better, more strategic approach might be to learn about their prospects' problems and offer tailored solutions. Having that balance between thinking and doing is very powerful.

In my signature book *Strategic Acceleration* (Perseus 2010), I introduced the concept of strategic beliefs—knowing the difference between strategic and tactical issues. By the time I wrote *RESULTS Faster!* in 2016 I had expanded that teaching to what I now call *Strategic IQ*—knowing and managing what percentage of the time you are operating in the tactical (activities like tasks, calls, and paperwork) and what percentage you operate in the strategic (planning, thinking, and studying).

You're more prepared to solve problems effectively if you understand the *Strategic IQ* model and are balancing your efforts between the two. Sometimes your efforts may need to be tactical, when you need to get down into your action plan, and sometimes you may need

THE MORE PREPARED
YOU ARE TO LIVE IN
SOLUTIONS, THE MORE
NATURALLY STRATEGIC
YOU'LL BECOME, AND THIS
CAN HAVE A DRAMATIC
IMPACT ON YOUR
RESULTS.

to be lifting up and strategically looking at the big picture. The more prepared you are to live in solutions, the more naturally strategic you'll become, and this can have a dramatic impact on your results.

18.
Execute with Accountability

How do you get the right results faster, with powerful accountability? You have to execute!

As you prepare ahead for success, keep this critical fact in mind: You can create the greatest plan in the world and establish the most focused goals imaginable, and yet if you fail to execute the plan you will not achieve it.

As I see it, there are two huge culprits when it comes to failing to execute well:

1. The biggest culprit, by far, is a communication disconnect between those who conceive the vision and those who must turn it into reality. You must start with what I call *Strategic Clarity* about your vision—understand what you really want, why you want it, the value of doing it, and the highest purpose for doing it. Then you must be able to specifically communicate the "why" of it to those you need to work with to execute the vision, whether that's to a large group or a small group of people.

> YOU CAN CREATE THE GREATEST PLAN IN THE WORLD AND ESTABLISH THE MOST FOCUSED GOALS IMAGINABLE, AND YET IF YOU FAIL TO EXECUTE THE PLAN YOU WILL NOT ACHIEVE IT.

2. The second reason people often fail to execute well is that they fail to measure. Peter Drucker is credited with saying, "What gets measured gets improved." Accountability comes with measuring. If you want to move to the mastery level of getting results, you need to take this distinction to heart. **Prepare ahead on how you're going to measure, and then measure everything.** For example, remember what I talked about in No. 14, "Focus on Results Versus Activity." Look at your to-do list every

morning and then again many times throughout the day, and then again in the evening, to measure what you got accomplished. Know what matters and why, and then make sure you focus on your HLAs and eliminate your LLAs.

PREPARE AHEAD ON HOW YOU'RE GOING TO MEASURE, AND THEN MEASURE EVERYTHING.

19.
UNDERSTAND THAT SPEED MATTERS

Speed is part of my brand. I've invested decades of my life into helping high achievers get focused on growing their business success faster.

Business is a results contest, and that typically involves a great deal of competition. My company recently made a video clip called "Life is Fast" (do a search for "Tony Jeary Life is Fast"). We live in a fast-paced world, where people want things quickly. They buy from the business that delivers their products better and faster. Speed is everything, and you must keep up the pace in order to win. One of the main reasons for that kind of demand from consumers is that Amazon has changed the world's expectations. People are saying, "Why would I want to shop anywhere else if I can just go on the internet and buy it? And if I can go on the internet and just hit one button to buy it, that's even better."

> SPEED IS EVERYTHING, AND YOU MUST KEEP UP THE PACE IN ORDER TO WIN.

The more prepared you are, the easier you can get things done faster and meet the world's expectations. Successful people know the outcomes (the right results) they need in advance, and they also know how to make them happen. They have three strategic distinctions that produce the right results faster:

1. They have clarity about what they want.

2. They know how to focus on doing the things that matter.

3. They know how to execute their plans and achieve their goals.

How about you? How do you rate yourself on those three distinctions? Constantly be asking yourself, *How can I be more prepared?*

20.
MOVE TO MASTERY BY USING INTENTIONAL SELF-TALK

In the lesson on Preparation in my *RESULTS Faster!* book, I listed six ways to make preparation a secret to your success. Number four on that list was self-talk—constantly asking the powerful question, *What can I do to be ready?*

You may be saying to yourself right now, *I don't really do self-talk.* Well, guess what! That's self-talk. We all talk to ourselves. So while you're at it, ask yourself, *What can I do to be ready—and not just ready, but super ready? Is there anything else I can remember?* (I suggest you don't say, *I don't want to forget this,* because that's a negative embedded command. Make it positive.)

One mistake I made for many years was not appreciating my self-talk. Since I want to be the best I can be mentally each time I go on stage, I now remind myself about the number of miles I've travelled, the number of sessions I've taught, and the number of talks I've given across the world. Then my mind thinks, *Okay, you've done this for over twenty-five years, and this presentation will be as impactful as always. Go out there and be your natural self and impact.* By employing that kind of intentional self-talk—often combined with a prayer that I will be valuable for my audience and not be stuck on being perfect—I can be more into being myself. I've had to learn to be that specific in my self-talk, because for years it was all about how I could look good, versus putting all my energy into presenting so my audience could get the most out of it. Now, I'm certainly not saying that we don't want to look good. It's just that the intentional self-talk I've learned is more focused on how I can impact my audiences.

> CONSTANTLY ASK YOURSELF THE POWERFUL QUESTION, WHAT CAN I DO TO BE READY—AND NOT JUST READY, BUT SUPER READY?

Here are some other ways you can use self-talk to move toward mastery:

1. Managing stress. You have to use self-talk here and ask yourself, *Does it really matter?* It was a habit I had to get into.

2. Preventing negative procrastination (putting things off when you shouldn't). Think about your self-talk right now. Is it giving you legitimate reasons to put things off? Really, all procrastination comes back to self-talk. Sometimes we say things like, *Oh, it doesn't really matter. I'll do that later. No one cares.* Or sometimes we may say, *You know, I just don't feel like doing that right now.* That's negative procrastination.

    A legitimate thing to say to ourselves, when it's true, may be, *I need to take a little bit of time to gain some more valuable insights before I make that decision.* That's positive and *Strategic Procrastination.* Even if you say, I need to sleep on it tonight, because you know you'll make a better decision if you let your intuition work throughout the evening and night, that's positive procrastination.

    To gain results, you need to take charge of your time and your life. Here are a few examples of possible ways to contradict negative self-talk.

- *I can do it tomorrow.* Ask yourself, *What can I get started on now that will help me complete this project and help the others who are waiting for me?*

- *I don't have everything I need, so I'll wait.* Ask yourself, *What can I do now, with what I have on hand?*

- *I can't do it perfectly (or, I need to do more research), so I'll wait.* See No. 26, "Have a Do-It-Now Mindset," where we talk about my idea of *Production Before Perfection.*

- *I don't have time right now.* Ask yourself, *What can I do in the next five (ten, fifteen, or twenty) minutes that will move me toward the results I want?*

- *Someone else can do it better.* Say to yourself, *Even if someone else can do this better, it's my task and my responsibility. I may even get better as I keep working on this!*

- *I just don't feel like it right now.* Many people find that getting started is the biggest hurdle. Say to yourself, *I'll just do five (ten, fifteen, or twenty) minutes of work on this.* You'll see that you often get caught up in the task and make tremendous progress.

3. Avoiding sabotaging your goals. Use positive self-talk that's congruent with your goals. For example, if your goal is to be organized and you say things like, *Well, you know, I'm not a very organized person,* then you have self-sabotaged. You need to be saying positive things like, *I'm getting more organized so I can reach my goals.*

21.
BE INTENTIONAL ABOUT EVERYTHING

Intentionality starts with clarity, and yet it's more than clarity or focus because it centers around action, not just thought. To become exceptional, you must be intentional about every action. When you're in tune with your values and you're clear about the values you live by, you can become more intentional about every aspect of your life.

- To prepare ahead in business, you should have well-thought-out and documented standards, based on what you want and what you don't want.

- If a big part of your success is the people around you, then make sure you're ready for success by replacing those who aren't right for you with some who are.

- Be intentional about who you spend time with. Hang around others who match your values. Prepare with mental clarity, and then say "yes" or "no" accordingly.

> WHEN YOU ARE IN TUNE WITH YOUR VALUES AND YOU KNOW THE VALUES YOU LIVE BY, YOU BECOME MORE INTENTIONAL ABOUT EVERY ASPECT OF YOUR LIFE.

- Be intentional about how much stress you can manage, including how many projects you can take on.

- Think before you do anything. Be strategic; then do things fast, and your energy and resources will be expended and utilized in the best way.

- Take time to identify the qualities and characteristics you like about yourself—your natural talents and strengths—so you can become much more intentional about the pathways you take.

In whatever you're doing, strategically ask yourself, *Will this produce the result I'm after, or do I need to go deeper?* Are you shooting for a short-term result, a medium-term result, a long-term, or all three? I think that applies in marriage, it applies in negotiation, and it applies in everyday business life.

Intentionality exists when you know exactly what you want, and everything flows from that. First you must know what you really want. Then you can be intentional about taking action.

IN WHATEVER YOU'RE DOING, STRATEGICALLY ASK YOURSELF, WILL THIS PRODUCE THE RESULT I'M AFTER, OR DO I NEED TO GO DEEPER?

22.
ADHERE TO THE 140-PERCENT RULE (DON'T OVERDO)

Prepare by first becoming aware of expectations, and then be so clear on them that you know when you're ahead.

There's a saying that goes, **"Excellence adds value; perfection just adds time."** Many people strive for perfection to such a degree that they either stop because they can never seem to reach their desired state, or they put in significantly more time than there is value to receive.

As you may know, my business mantra is "Give value; do more than is expected." The mental target is about 110 percent, and I apply that to virtually everything I do. Do enough to exceed expectations; however, don't overdo it (say, to 140 percent). Doing so takes energy and effort from other projects, goals, and even tasks you can be accomplishing.

Striving for perfection can sidetrack your results and make your customers or clients wait. They want results, and they want them fast. Remember, speed is everything. Focusing on perfection can often cause analysis paralysis, where people lose more than they win.

EXCELLENCE ADDS VALUE; PERFECTION JUST ADDS TIME. MANY PEOPLE STRIVE FOR PERFECTION TO SUCH A DEGREE THAT THEY EITHER STOP BECAUSE THEY CAN NEVER SEEM TO REACH THEIR DESIRED STATE, OR THEY PUT IN SIGNIFICANTLY MORE TIME THAN THERE IS VALUE TO RECEIVE.

23.
CHANNEL YOUR EMOTIONS AND CONTROL YOUR EGO

Living a well-managed life includes managing your emotions and all of the inner workings of your mind. How well do you manage your emotions?

I suggest you listen and think before you do. Dale Carnegie's book *How to Win Friends and Influence People* has had a huge impact on my life since my girlfriend's father gave me a copy when I was sixteen years old. One of the top thirty principles in that book is listening. I've discovered that you can control both your emotions and your ego much better if you're listening to the other person and preparing for and thinking about how that person can win.

LISTEN AND THINK BEFORE YOU DO.

I've authored several books on Neuro-Linguistic Programming (NLP) and I just completed another small book called *Understanding the Power of NLP.* One of the most effective concepts of NLP is communicating with people according to their map versus your map. Let me explain:

A core of NLP is the understanding that everyone sees the world differently. We all see the world through our own unique experiences, culture, language, beliefs, values, interests, and assumptions. Each of us lives in our own distinct reality, built from our own impressions and individual experiences of life, and we act on the basis of what we perceive our model of the world to be. In other words, the variety of our experiences from the time we're born creates principles and truisms that become our "map," or what I refer to often as our *Belief Window,* through which we filter the world (the "territory") and make our choices.

Preparing ahead by understanding NLP can help you manage your internal state (emotions), and it can give you a high degree of behavioral flexibility in difficult situations. I look at NLP as a magic language that helps us better communicate with others. The more we understand how people see the world through their own filters, the more easily we

PREPARING AHEAD BY UNDERSTANDING NLP CAN HELP YOU MANAGE YOUR INTERNAL STATE (EMOTIONS), AND IT CAN GIVE YOU A HIGH DEGREE OF BEHAVIORAL FLEXIBILITY IN DIFFICULT SITUATIONS.

can guide them toward better outcomes. By using NLP to see the world the way they see it, we can create wins for people by influencing them with integrity.

When most people communicate, they're communicating through their own window (map) and not thinking about the windows of the people they're taking to, and then they wonder why their message isn't being received well. That's when ego and emotions can flare. When you want someone to be very receptive to the message you're sharing, you need to mentally prepare and think about how they see the world. A good general rule of thumb is to be thinking about other people and not so much yourself, and then most of the time your message will be much better received.

Sometimes your ego wants to win more than you want the other person to win. Do you want to win at all costs? Often you can be so much better prepared if you step back and let them win, even if they may not be right. Which do you want more—to win more or to have greater relationships?

In life and relationships, emotions and ego are always a factor. How well you control those things can impact your ability to connect with others and persuade them to see things the way you need them to in order to achieve predetermined results. Sometimes we don't see that our own emotions are creating destructive results. They could be getting in the way of bonding with colleagues, attracting new clients, or closing deals. Learning to separate emotion from business decisions will help you accelerate your results.

IV. TIME MINDSET

Learn to enjoy every minute of your life.
Be happy now. Don't wait for something outside of yourself
to make you happy in the future. Think how really precious
is the time you have to spend, whether it's at work or with your family.
Every minute should be enjoyed and savored.
—EARL NIGHTINGALE

Time is more value than money. You can get more money,
but you cannot get more time.
—JIM ROHN

The future is something that everyone reaches at the rate of sixty
minutes an hour, whatever he does, whoever he is.
—C.S. LEWIS

24.
THE MORE TIME YOU SAVE, THE MORE YOU HAVE TO INVEST ELSEWHERE

Time is an equalizer; we all have the same amount. No one has enough, yet everyone has all there is. Poor time management—not being clear and focusing on your *High Leverage Activities* (see No. 13)—will put you in a position where you're not optimizing, either in your preparation or your execution.

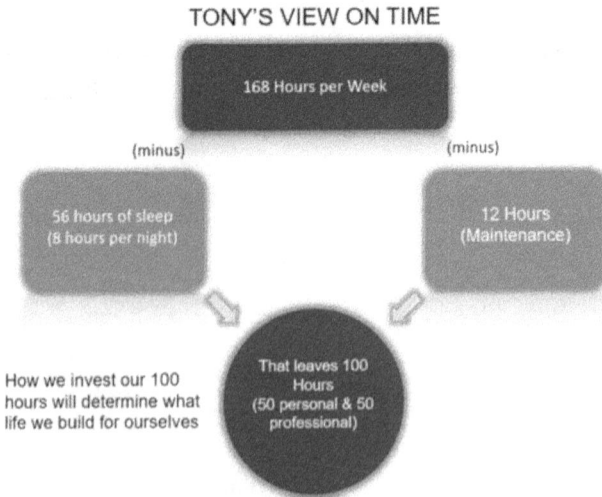

> POOR TIME MANAGEMENT—NOT BEING CLEAR AND FOCUSING ON YOUR HIGH LEVERAGE ACTIVITIES—WILL PUT YOU IN A POSITION WHERE YOU'RE NOT OPTIMIZING, EITHER IN YOUR PREPARATION OR YOUR EXECUTION.

Time is extremely valuable. Think about the 168 hours we have in a week, with 100 left to invest after deducting hours for sleep and maintenance. (See my model below.) Most of us invest about 50 hours in our professional lives and 50 in our personal lives, and how we use those hours in both areas (how well we focus on our HLAs) determines our success. It can make the difference in winning and losing.

TONY'S VIEW ON TIME

168 Hours per Week

(minus)

(minus)

56 hours of sleep
(8 hours per night)

12 Hours
(Maintenance)

How we invest our 100 hours will determine what life we build for ourselves

That leaves 100 Hours
(50 personal & 50 professional)

25.
Practice Delayed Gratification as a Master Principle of Winning

You can have anything you want. You just can't have everything at once!

High achievers often focus on immediate results so they can see, experience, and achieve results quickly. I get it; we all want results now. We're all tempted to invest our resources in things that provide immediate payoff; however, if we want to prepare well for the future, we should also focus our efforts on things that pay off down the road. If all our efforts were rewarded short term, we could be missing out on what matters most.

> IF ALL OUR EFFORTS WERE REWARDED SHORT TERM, WE COULD BE MISSING OUT ON WHAT MATTERS MOST.

If you try to tackle every opportunity that comes your way all at once, you could lose your focus and invest way too much time trying to keep up with everything. A lot of business people lose their drive, their health, and then their marriages because they can't say "no." Think about this: Are you spending your health for wealth? I did for a while, and then I woke up! I don't have to have everything—at least not all right now. Life is a journey, and we need to do our best to live it that way.

One smart strategy to achieve what you want without overload—and without taxing your resources—is to stage your successes, purchases, and big spends. Differentiate between your needs versus your wants. You can delay gratification and plan things far into the future, and they will mean even more because you planned for them. Timing is everything.

Give yourself a reality check and consider whether you really need everything right now, all at once. Focus on what you really want to have, share, experience, and become. Know what you want, and have complete clarity about how to bring it into your world so it compliments—

not complicates—your life.

Have the discipline to wisely delay gratification and build future wins. Think about what you should invest in now that will pay off later relative to your kids, your home, your financial stability, your health, your brand, and your business. Make a plan, get clear on your goals, and start thinking, organizing, and building for future rewards. Be intentional about doing now what will pay big dividends later.

Here are a few suggestions for things to invest in now that will result in a huge payoff later:

FOCUS ON WHAT YOU REALLY WANT TO HAVE, SHARE, EXPERIENCE, AND BECOME. KNOW WHAT YOU WANT, AND HAVE COMPLETE CLARITY ABOUT HOW TO BRING IT INTO YOUR WORLD SO IT COMPLIMENTS— NOT COMPLICATES— YOUR LIFE.

- Invest time in building memories, not just making money.
- Invest in yourself (prepare for peak performance) with rest and sleep so your body can rebuild each day.
- Invest in physicals and preventative health.
- Invest in your goals, your vision, your marriage, and your relationships.

Plant seeds now to see them bloom for years to come.

26.
HAVE A "DO-IT-NOW" MINDSET

Prepare for success by leading a no-excuses life. When you put things off—intentionally or not—you often end up stressed, without the right resources, and behind on time commitments. The killer here is often perfectionism, which is one of the biggest causes of procrastination. (Note: Preparation is powerful and is a necessary step; and yet if you're not careful, over preparation could become a form of procrastination.)

PREPARE FOR SUCCESS BY LEADING A NO-EXCUSES LIFE.

Production Before Perfection (PBP) helps you burst through procrastination. For some people, this can be the most important of all my time management concepts. Many people allow perfectionism (the fear of imperfection) to stop them from starting on a project. It's often best to jump in and make things happen first, and then you can perfect as you go.

PBP is a concept I developed a long time ago, and our clients love it. It applies to most people, and that may include you. It's the whole idea that *now* matters—get it done *now*. Many people don't get that. They offer up excuses for why they can't or won't get started. Are you an excuse person, or are you a results person? How many tasks are you procrastinating on right now because you want them to be too perfect?

Let me give you an example: Are taxes something that need to be perfect, or if not perfect, pretty close? Yes. Then does that mean you have to wait to get started on them until you get every 1099 OR W-2 or investment document together? No, you can start working on your taxes each month of the year, by keeping track of your taxable expenses and being organized about keeping receipts.

NOW MATTERS—GET IT DONE NOW!

Now, there are a few exceptions where PBP would not be practical. If you're building a helicopter, you don't want to send someone into the air unless it's pretty perfect. Right? Or if you're a scientist, or maybe a doctor performing surgery, you want everything to be as perfect

MANY PEOPLE ALLOW PERFECTIONISM (THE FEAR OF IMPERFECTION) TO STOP THEM FROM STARTING ON A PROJECT. IT'S OFTEN BEST TO JUMP IN AND MAKE THINGS HAPPEN FIRST, AND THEN YOU CAN PERFECT AS YOU GO.

as it can be. For most people, though, whatever they're doing doesn't have to be perfect—maybe an 8 or a 9, or a 9.5. Get going, and then make it better as you go!

I've found that the higher a person's self-esteem, the more they accept responsibility and the less excuses they have, because they take ownership of their work. Those who have a lower self-esteem often put their work off for someone else.

27.
SAY "NO" STRATEGICALLY (AND STILL GIVE PEOPLE WHAT THEY WANT)

Learning to say "no" strategically is one of the best ways you can prepare for success. Saying "no" to low leverage activities frees you up and allows you to be more prepared to focus on HLA opportunities. So how do you say "no" strategically? By making a habit of evaluating everything according to your HLAs. You should say "yes" very rarely, and only when the opportunity matches your priorities, and "no" to anything else. When you say "yes" to something that's not related to your HLAs, you're saying "no" to something that is. Are you saying "no" enough? In my opinion, that's the most important word there is in regard to productivity!

> SAY "NO" STRATEGICALLY BY MAKING A HABIT OF EVALUATING EVERYTHING ACCORDING TO YOUR HLAS.

I state with complete conviction that saying "no" is an overlooked secret to success. In today's fast-paced world, we're presented with opportunities almost every waking minute. There are commercials, messages, products, emails, phone calls, offers, meetings, and activities of all kinds bombarding us from all sides. Since most people don't know how to deal with them effectively, they don't say "no" enough. Does that include you?

If you understand this one thing, you will be shocked at how much more time you will find in your day, week, and month to prepare for and execute your HLAs. You'll have more choices to do what matters the most if you understand that you must say "no" to the things that don't matter. This is a magic rule; it takes discipline and good thinking to a whole new level.

Let me give you an example of what saying "no" strategically looks like. Let's say Doug, who is an acquaintance, asks me to go to

> SAYING "NO" IS AN OVERLOOKED SECRET TO SUCCESS.

lunch. The first thing I would do is ask myself, *Does going to lunch with Doug tie in with one of my HLAs?* If it doesn't, then I have to make a choice—and the smart choice would be to ask Doug what he wants. He may say something like, "Well, I want to talk about having you come and speak for my event. We don't have a budget, so we were hoping you would come and speak for free." What he really wants to do, obviously, is take me to lunch and talk me into speaking. I get requests like that often, as you can imagine, so I might say something like, "My calendar stays full respecting my team and my family, so I'll need to pass. However, since you're a non-profit, why don't I send you fifty complimentary books for your people?" I strategically said "no" and saved myself time; and yet, because I'd prepared ahead and had an arsenal of books, I could give Doug something of value that he wants.

People usually don't say "no" because they don't know how, they don't want to miss out on anything, or they don't want to offend someone. People pleasers struggle here; they're rarely wildly successful if they don't master this one. If you don't learn how to say "no," needless activities can pile up on your calendar, draining valuable time from important projects and goals—valuable moments from your life that you'll never get back.

> SUCCESSFUL BUSINESSES ARE BUILT WHEN CLARITY, FOCUS, AND EXECUTION CONVERGE OVER AND OVER AGAIN.

Saying "no" is empowering. It helps build your self-esteem, reduces stress, and gives you more time and energy. Successful businesses are not built on a feeling of obligation or a fear of saying "no." Successful businesses are built when clarity, focus, and execution converge over and over again.

28.
CREATE ELEGANT SOLUTIONS

Creating *Elegant Solutions* is an excellent way to jumpstart your level of preparedness. *Elegant Solutions* are created when you have such extreme clarity (similar to a helicopter view) on what you want to accomplish that you can intentionally achieve multiple objectives with a single action or effort.

Elegant Solutions are a powerful way to leverage your time and efforts. When you're really clear on your vision and your goals and objectives and you keep them in front of you every day, you can continually think of ways to create *Elegant Solutions* and accomplish several objectives at one time. The time it takes to think about and prepare for them pays off handsomely in the end.

> WHEN YOU'RE REALLY CLEAR ON YOUR VISION AND YOUR GOALS AND OBJECTIVES AND YOU KEEP THEM IN FRONT OF YOU EVERY DAY, YOU CAN CONTINUALLY THINK OF WAYS TO CREATE *ELEGANT SOLUTIONS* AND ACCOMPLISH SEVERAL OBJECTIVES AT ONE TIME.

For example, when I travel, I'll often think strategically about who can travel with me, what objectives we can accomplish, who else we can meet while we're there, what kind of memories and/or learning we can create, and where we can stay that will have the biggest impact and align with my goals, and then I prepare accordingly. I just came back from Mexico, where I ended up accomplishing six or eight additional objectives while I was enjoying a vacation with my family. Here are a few of my strategically planned and prepared *Elegant Solutions*:

• I put my future son-in-law in the same room with my current son-in-law to see how they would connect and to see how he would fit in as a potential new family member. (I'm happy to report that it worked out great.)

- I put my two daughters together in the same room so they could have extra time together.

- While I was out enjoying the sunshine by the pool I was also preparing for our excursions, taking care of a few items of business on my phone, etc.

Here's another one of my *Elegant Solutions* I employ on a regular basis: In order to maximize my time, I've had a driver for twenty years who drives me to meetings and to and from the airport so I can attend to such business activities in the back seat as conducting conference calls, taking notes, or reading—all while I'm accomplishing the objective of getting to wherever I need to go.

Here are some other examples of *Elegant Solutions*:

- Invite someone you're mentoring (or perhaps a new team member) to participate in a meeting that would add value to them and teach them, simultaneously.

- Take your kids on a business trip with you to help them learn (and prepare for life) and invest time together while you're working.

- Plan a business lunch or happy hour at a popular networking spot and perhaps connect with others at the same time.

- Select places to vacation where your family can learn a new culture or experience something new, while also spending quality time together. Talk about your goals on the trip. (We did all this during our recent vacation in Mexico.)

WHAT YOU DO WITH YOUR TIME DETERMINES WHAT YOU DO WITH YOUR LIFE.

- Host an event that both brings value to your clients and connects them with others who can bring value to them.

- Work out with a business colleague or client.

Creating *Elegant Solutions* leads to multiple wins. **What you do with your time determines what you do with your life.** Begin to rethink your time habits and better understand how the time investment choices you make (including preparation) really affect the results you seek. Then work to create *Elegant Solutions* that allow you to accomplish more in the same amount of time.

29.
APPRECIATE AND INVEST TIME IN WHAT YOU WANT MORE OF

When you're thinking about how to prepare for the best results, this is a very important principle: Appreciate what you want more of in every area of your life. And that certainly

Time is precious because we only have so much of it, so we need to make sure we're investing it wisely into the things that matter. To me, that means we have to prepare really strategically and make every minute count. The clearer you are on what you want, the more you can put your time into the things that are important to you.

In No. 11 we talked about doing a MOLO audit of your life to determine what you want more of and what you want less of. Once you've determined what you want more of, start strategically appreciating and investing time in those things.

> PREPARE REALLY STRATEGICALLY AND MAKE EVERY MINUTE COUNT. THE CLEARER YOU ARE ON WHAT YOU WANT, THE MORE YOU CAN PUT YOUR TIME INTO THE THINGS THAT ARE IMPORTANT TO YOU.

This concept applies even to what you say or write on any given day. For years I have sent texts to my girls almost daily (even after they became young adults) appreciating them for making good decisions. I've prepared them for years, and they are now incredible young women who make exceptional decisions. When you verbally appreciate something specific, people want to do more of it. It's that simple.

Our families are one of God's greatest gifts. We are charged with the responsibility of nurturing family relationships, with the overall goal of creating happy, secure, and successful families. The common threads of faithfulness and commitment hold successful families together, for those attributes create an atmosphere of love and trust in which families

80

WHEN YOU VERBALLY APPRECIATE SOMETHING SPECIFIC, PEOPLE WANT TO DO MORE OF IT. IT'S THAT SIMPLE.

can thrive. If you want a great family, invest in them and appreciate them, a lot! Likewise, if you want a healthy company or a healthy body, invest in them and the results will multiply.

30.
PRIORITIZE HOURLY

Ask yourself hourly, *What's the best use of my time right now?* I think about that question eight, ten, or twelve times a day, and you should too. Having the discipline to do that is a very powerful preparation tool that I would encourage you to put into your habits.

In No. 13, we talked about focusing on your *High Leverage Activities* (HLAs)—those activities that have the most impact on moving the needle toward your goals—and we talked about developing a habit of saying "no" to most things that are not on your HLA list. If you want to prepare yourself to say "no" to what's not mission-critical (distractions) and "yes" to those important activities that are focused on helping you reach your goals, continually ask yourself, *What's the best use of my time right now?* and then prioritize accordingly. Forming the habit of doing this effectively will serve you in leading your best life.

> ASK YOURSELF EIGHT, TEN, OR TWELVE TIMES A DAY, WHAT IS THE BEST USE OF MY TIME RIGHT NOW?

Priorities may shift by the hour, or even by the minute. I was recently scheduled for a conference call to talk with one of my writers about this book, and I had a variety of different things happen that required shifting my time. I had to delay the call by six minutes and change some other things to that afternoon, because something went over that morning that was really positive. I'm constantly assessing and prioritizing my schedule, because things change. I can prepare myself for that kind of flexibility by asking myself, *What's the best use of my time right now?* Then, if something comes up that trumps what I'm doing, I can adjust it.

V. THINKING

The world as we have created it is a process of our thinking.
It cannot be changed without changing our thinking.
—ALBERT EINSTEIN

You control your future, your destiny. What you think about comes
about. By recording your dreams and goals on paper, you set in motion
the process of becoming the person you most want to be.
Put your future in good hands—your own.
—MARK VICTOR HANSEN

Whether you think you can, or you think you can't—you're right.
—HENRY FORD

31.
YOU BECOME WHAT
YOU THINK ABOUT

Prepare for a most wonderful life by thinking about your values, your purpose, and your goals, and make thinking an intentional habit.

[Callout:]

Earl Nightingale wrote *The Strangest Secret,* considered one of the greatest motivational books of all time. What was his "strangest secret"? **You become what you think about.** Nightingale claimed that only 5 percent of the people in the world achieve success, simply because of the way they think. People who set goals succeed because they know where they are going. They have planted their goals in their mind.

PREPARE FOR A MOST WONDERFUL LIFE BY THINKING ABOUT YOUR VALUES, YOUR PURPOSE, AND YOUR GOALS, AND MAKE THINKING AN INTENTIONAL HABIT.

That is precisely why I preach and teach thinking and author so many works on the subject. Thinking matters much more than people believe it does. Many just keep working away at their to-do list, versus really thinking about the right things they should be doing.

When I was a young man preparing for my future, I said I wanted to become one of the most valuable advisors in the world. I established that as my vision, set my goals toward it, created an action plan, and started doing the things that would move the needle in that direction.

One the ways I prepared for it was by authoring over fifty books for my tool box over a period of a couple of decades. During that time I also built a track record with an arsenal of high-achieving clients, travelling millions of miles to work with over 1,000 clients in more than fifty countries. I hired tons of people to make me smarter, and I read hundreds of books and did a great deal of research. I've achieved that vision because I was willing to think about it ahead of time and prepare

CHANGE YOUR
THINKING,
CHANGE YOUR
RESULTS.

for success with all the things I've done for the past thirty years.

My tag line is "Change your thinking, change your results." Decide now what you want and plant that goal in your mind. Then be *Intentionally Strategic* (cast deliberate and calculated thinking toward your purpose, your goals, and your objectives) about everything you do, and that will lead to the results you're looking for.

32.
FIND GREAT MENTORS OR COACHES

Advice Matters. I believe that so much that I coauthored a book by that name several years ago. If you want to really be ahead of the game as you prepare for your future, arrange to get advice from those who have done what you want to do. Ask that they share their learnings with you so you can enhance your decision-making effectiveness.

Seeking advice from others who have achieved the kind of results you're looking for is one of the wisest and quickest ways to design, prepare for, and live a successful life, grow your business, and hit that next level of success. In fact, seeking advice is often the crucial piece of the success puzzle that catapults your results into an arena you could never have achieved alone.

> SEEKING ADVICE IS OFTEN THE CRUCIAL PIECE OF THE SUCCESS PUZZLE THAT CATAPULTS YOUR RESULTS TO AN ARENA YOU COULD NEVER HAVE ACHIEVED ALONE.

Learning from the experiences of others, both their mistakes and their successes, helps you think better and thus leads to your making better decisions and creating a better business and a better life. Wise advice can also help you avoid pitfalls that could derail your success. Prepare for extraordinary results by seeking advice from people who have produced extraordinary results.

If you want different results, you need new thinking—it's that simple! If you act alone, you can only be as successful as your own mind allows you to be. New information stimulates both your reasoning processes and your creative juices and helps you think better. Learning strategically from the wisdom and insight of others helps you be more successful *faster*. Remember, in today's market speed often is your competitive advantage and directly impacts your ability to compete and win.

A mentor is someone who is willing to give you advice about how to run your business, attract more clients, or implement certain valuable processes, and they offer their wisdom for free. I have personally benefited immensely from several mentor-mentee relationships. For example, I wanted to raise exceptional kids, so I found mentors who had already achieved that. I even found mentors who had two girls, just like I do. I carefully chose those mentors who had successful daughters and asked them to prepare me and my wife for parenting by sharing their knowledge and time with us. As a result, I have two incredible young adult daughters who are both making the world a better place. It really is valuable to get the opinion and insight of others who are equally committed to your success.

I call coaching the "secret weapon of many of the world's top achievers." Few people automatically understand what it takes to prepare for success, reach their goals, overcome their weaknesses, and grow their strengths. One-on-one coaching can advance your career, grow your leadership skills, help you build your brand, and uncover *Blind Spots*. The right coach can take you to the next level, where you see a significant increase in your income, reach your goals faster, and become stronger in all areas of your life.

THE RIGHT COACH CAN TAKE YOU TO THE NEXT LEVEL, WHERE YOU SEE A SIGNIFICANT INCREASE IN YOUR INCOME, REACH YOUR GOALS FASTER, AND BECOME STRONGER IN ALL AREAS OF YOUR LIFE.

When you connect with the right coach for you, it's an investment—not an expense—and it should pay short, medium, and long–term dividends. The right coach should dramatically alter the results of your life.

I think one *Blind Spot* most people have is they don't have a mentor, and the second *Blind Spot* is they don't have multiple mentors. The third *Blind Spot* many have is they don't understand that you can pay your coach to be your mentor, and smart coaches bring tool boxes and connections to the table.

You can prepare well for your future if you're willing to take advice.

33.
USE PLANNED SPONTANEITY

Planned Spontaneity is being so prepared and so ready that you can spontaneously operate smoothly, easily, and effortlessly in every situation.

Working to be perfect is not the right goal and is seldom the best way to reach your presentation objective(s). *Planned Spontaneity* is what works best. The better prepared you are, the more spontaneity you can easily bring to your meetings and presentations with confidence, and the more you can actually relax, flow, and move naturally in the moment. When an audience member asks a question that is not covered in your planned remarks, you can access that information in your brain and answer the question with confidence, because you've researched and studied far beyond your planned remarks. You can go off track or off the planned agenda with ease and then move back on the track you planned.

> THE BETTER PREPARED YOU ARE, THE MORE SPONTANEITY YOU CAN EASILY BRING TO YOUR MEETINGS AND PRESENTATIONS WITH CONFIDENCE, AND THE MORE YOU CAN ACTUALLY RELAX, FLOW, AND MOVE NATURALLY IN THE MOMENT.

Planned Spontaneity is the quality that separates the master presenters from those who are merely good, because it allows you to spontaneously react to your attendees in a way that matters most to them. People really do prefer realism over perfectionism!

I believe *Planned Spontaneity* means preparing to the extreme, even to the point of making sure you get the right amount of rest, putting yourself in the right mental state, and doing everything you possibly can to be super ready. I've found that most people prepare for major events and opportunities, and yet few people prepare as strategically as they should, which includes the powerful mind shift we're suggesting here.

Something you may not realize is that life is a series of presentations. (I wrote a book by that name, as well.) You're presenting with every phone call, email, text, and conversation where your goal is to persuade someone to do something. With *Planned Spontaneity* you can be so prepared for anything that you're set up for maximum flexibility. Plan ahead so you're ready for virtually anything.

PLANNED SPONTANEITY IS THE QUALITY THAT SEPARATES THE MASTER PRESENTERS FROM THOSE WHO ARE MERELY GOOD, BECAUSE IT ALLOWS YOU TO SPONTANEOUSLY REACT TO YOUR ATTENDEES IN A WAY THAT MATTERS MOST TO THEM.

34.
Develop Sensory Acuity

Take preparation to the next level by developing something called sensory acuity, which is the skill of using all your senses to observe distinctions. Sensory acuity is an NLP concept that can be particularly useful in watching out for potential threats, land minds, or things that can go wrong. Strategically using your mind and all five senses—what you smell, hear, taste, see, and experience— to catch all the right details can also help you know what actions to take (or whether to take no action at all).

Being acutely aware positions you to better prepare, because it

BEING ACUTELY AWARE POSITIONS YOU TO BETTER PREPARE, BECAUSE IT HELPS YOU DECIDE WHAT TO YOU WANT TO AVOID, DUPLICATE, MODEL, OR UTILIZE. BY INTENTIONALLY ACTIVATING YOUR FIVE SENSES, YOU CAN MENTALLY INCREASE YOUR ABILITY TO QUESTION, OBSERVE, OR NOTICE DISTINCTIONS.

helps you decide what to you want to avoid, duplicate, model, or utilize. By intentionally activating your five senses, you can mentally increase your ability to question, observe, or notice distinctions.

For example, if you want to duplicate a person's closing ratio, notice all their subtleties, including speed, word choices, order, volume, environmental details, etc. When you're talking to a prospect, spouse, child, friend, etc., become acutely aware of their word choices, their personality style, and their priorities. Personally, when I make phone calls, I almost always take notes myself and also have a staff member on the line taking notes as well, to further ensure that we catch all the distinctions. That way, two people are being acutely aware, and we compare notes and end up with a special level of details; hence, I have a better understanding and am positioned to communicate back more effectively.

35.
PREPARE WITH STATE MANAGEMENT

PUTTING YOURSELF IN THE RIGHT EMOTIONAL STATE TO PREPARE YOU FOR WHATEVER YOU NEED TO DO TO GET THE OUTCOME YOU WANT IS SO POWERFUL.

State management, another NLP concept, is preparing your mind to be in the right state for whatever important task is at hand. Putting yourself in the right emotional state to prepare you for whatever you need to do to get the outcome you want is so powerful.

Get yourself into the right frame of mind before making important calls, negotiating deals, and making powerful impressions. Positive thoughts bring positive results, a powerful state brings better results, and a resourceful state brings even better results.

For example, I often walk into my home gym and tell my Echo to play a certain song that will put me into the right emotional state to do a good training. I like to have my trainer there ahead of me, so when I walk in he already has my protein drink mixed and whatever I'm going to work on that day ready to go. All of that advance preparation puts me into a powerful state, ready to be my best.

POSITIVE THOUGHTS BRING POSITIVE RESULTS, A POWERFUL STATE BRINGS BETTER RESULTS, AND A RESOURCEFUL STATE BRINGS EVEN BETTER RESULTS.

36.
WAKE UP EARLY AND VISUALIZE YOUR DAY

Have you ever been wrestling to remember something, and it suddenly comes to you when you're first coming out of a deep sleep in the morning? That's because when you're waking up in the morning and coming out of a deep relaxation, your brain is in a frequency called alpha, which is the gateway to your subconscious mind.

Alpha is a relaxed, yet focused state of mind that allows you to be more receptive, open, and creative. When we utilize the alpha state, we have better memory and recall. Learning to access alpha at will can help sharpen your intuition; and if used on a regular basis—even for short periods—it can help you more easily cope with stress and reduce anxiety. And because you are calmer, you tend to be more prepared—you're more focused, make better decisions, and come to solutions faster.

LEARNING TO ACCESS ALPHA AT WILL CAN HELP SHARPEN YOUR INTUITION; AND IF USED ON A REGULAR BASIS—EVEN FOR SHORT PERIODS—IT CAN HELP YOU MORE EASILY COPE WITH STRESS AND REDUCE ANXIETY.

The next state is called beta, when your brain is coming into more of a waking consciousness and is in a heightened state of alertness, logic, and critical reasoning.

I've developed the habit of maximizing preparation for my day by getting up early after staying in bed an extra few minutes and playing out that alpha/beta state, so my unconscious mind can solve problems. Then, when I'm getting more into the beta state, I look at my phone. I do a lot of business around the world; and because the world travels about you even while you're sleeping, and because people often send me things at all hours of the night, I need to look at my phone to get a handle on my day. By that time my personal assistant has sent me

BRAIN MANAGEMENT

- Drop frequency (brain waves) down, get smoother brain function
- Subconscious is 100x more powerful than conscious
- Vision boards feed the subconscious

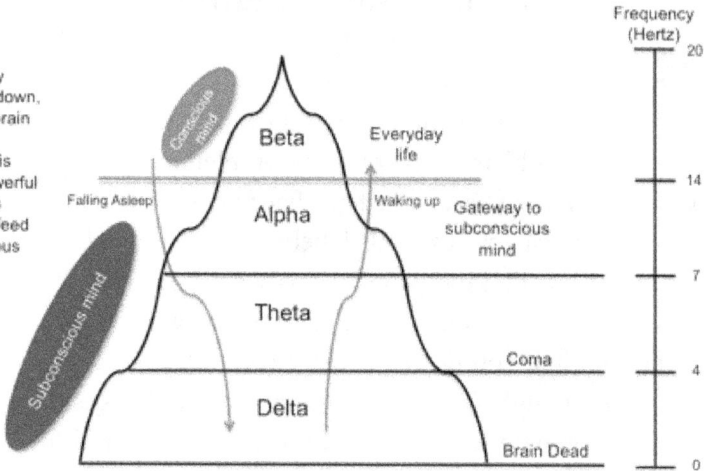

Frequency (Hertz)

Conscious mind

Subconscious mind

Beta — Everyday life

Falling Asleep

Alpha — Waking up — Gateway to subconscious mind

Theta

Coma

Delta

Brain Dead

20

14

7

4

0

TONY JEARY INTERNATIONAL
THE RESULTS GUY

WAKE UP EARLY, MAXIMIZE THE ALPHA AND BETA STATES OF YOUR BRAIN, AND VISUALIZE YOUR DAY SO YOU CAN PREPARE FOR THE RESULTS YOU WANT.

a snapshot of my calendar for the day and I start thinking about which meetings are the most important and visualizing the outcomes so I can be most prepared.

I encourage you to wake up early, maximize the alpha and beta states of your brain, and visualize your day so you can prepare for the results you want.

37.
VALUE DAILY THINKING TIME

High achievers want results. They want to win, and they're often faced with problems. One of those problems is that they want results faster. That may be what you're facing, as well. I believe every problem is a thinking problem. So what do you do when you don't get the results you want, or when you don't get the results you want fast enough? I suggest you make some changes. In fact, I suggest that you prepare for every day, for every week, and for the future by setting aside some time to think.

EVERY PROBLEM IS A THINKING PROBLEM.

One of my top CEO clients, whom I've coached for fifteen years, said to me a few years ago, "One of the things I want you to do is help my executives think more." He said "I want one of their *High Leverage Activities* to be thinking so we can go to another level." Here was a guy who had built a company to a billion dollars, and he valued having his executives think so much that he asked me to ensure they thought more! Well, I can tell you that it paid off—in a year and a half, the company's market capitalization went up over 30 percent—by $500 million dollars!

THINKING SHOULD BE AN HLA FOR ALL OF US.

Thinking is such a powerful piece of preparation, and most people don't do enough of it. It should be an HLA for all of us.

38.
Avoid Fear, Uncertainty, and Doubt

Think positive. That way you can prepare your mind to have your body get to work to win. Maintain clarity, stay focused on your goal, be persistent, and execute. Build, set up, and maintain a strong mental mindset so you're not spooked or shaken by fear, uncertainty, and doubt.

This is another powerful concept contributed by my fantastic coauthor Peter Thomas for our book *Business Ground Rules*. I'm going to recap that segment for you here.

WHEN WE GIVE INTO FEAR, UNCERTAINTY, AND DOUBT, WE SET OURSELVES UP FOR FAILURE.

Fear, uncertainty, and doubt (FUD) are three factors that inhibit most humans from reaching their goals and achieving their potential. When we give in to FUD, we set ourselves up for failure. And when we overcome FUD, we prepare ourselves for success. It's that simple.

Here's a personal story Peter shares in his *LifePilot* seminar that illustrates the way FUD can work and how you can overcome it:

When I was 35, I started buying the rights to Century 21 in Canada. I was excited and began to share my goal to do that with a business partner. The partner said it would never work; and when I asked him to invest money, he said no. So I went to another guy. He said it was a stupid idea. I asked my lawyer; he said no. Even my wife didn't think it was a good idea! The feedback I got ranged from, "It'll never work," to "No realtor is going to wear that gold jacket to work." (Century 21 had an interesting brand in which you could identify the realtors by their gold jackets.)

So at that time, I had really bought into the vision even though no one else around me had. I had a vision that no one else could see. I forged ahead despite the warnings and naysayers because I believed in it. And it was a success! I later sold it for $50 million. Sometimes everyone else is blind, when your vision is crystal clear.

In his early selling days, Peter always had a 4x6 card hanging from the rear-view window of his car. On the card was written in capital letters: "THIS WILL BE THE BEST PRESENTATION I HAVE EVER GIVEN." It was his reminder that he would not experience any fear, uncertainty, or doubt. Sure enough, every time he did a presentation, he made it the best presentation he had ever given. He had prepared himself for success!

It is so important to always give your best. Never allow yourself to give a mediocre performance, no matter what the circumstances, even if fear creeps in. Sometimes your best performances can come when it is most difficult for you to perform.

So what do you do if you start to feel a case of FUD coming on? The way to overcome it is to maintain clarity, stay focused on your goal, be persistent, and execute. Prepare yourself for success by not allowing fear, uncertainty, or doubt to rule your emotions, thoughts, or actions. If you really believe in something, keep doing it until you achieve your goal with a exceptional performance.

VI. RELATIONSHIPS

The very core of who we are is shaped by our relationships.
Great relationships can nourish our dreams, teach us true principles to
live by, and encourage us to grow and live life to the fullest.
—TONY JEARY

It is of practical value to learn to like yourself.
Since you spend so much time with yourself, you might as
well get some satisfaction out of the relationship.
—NORMAN VINCENT PEALE

Great companies that build an enduring brand have an emotional
relationship with customers that has no barrier. And that emotional
relationship is of the most important characteristic, which is trust.
—HOWARD SCHULTZ

39.
Build a Powerful Life Team

Prepare for future needs by building and nourishing a powerful and committed *Life Team*—people who help you extend your ability to get things done, make better decisions, and do life well.

Surrounding yourself with a hand-picked group of smart, talented individuals who have specific areas of expertise to leverage on your behalf is one of the best things you can do to prepare well for the future. They can be advisors (like attorneys, coaches, or mentors) or they can be doers (like electricians, landscapers, or CPAs). When you have a well-rounded *Life Team*, it's an easy matter to call someone who has the knowledge, expertise, or connections you need. You can also often rely on these people to do the things you are not good at or don't like to do, which allows you to better invest energy into doing the things you enjoy and excel in.

It's important to nourish your *Life Team* on an ongoing basis. Be a giver, and your *Life Team* members will serve you to a whole new level. I can call my drivers twenty-four hours a day and they'll do whatever I need—first because I picked the right team members, and second because I'm constantly showing how much I appreciate them. Just the other day I was online and saw a tool I didn't think they had, so I bought one for each of them. Most people who have a *Life Team* don't invest in them like they should.

If you want to be able to make things happen with one phone call, be intentional about:

1. Assembling a great team of people

2. Listing them on your phone for easy access

3. Constantly nourishing and appreciating them by doing things for them

40.
ESTABLISH AN INFORMAL BOARD OF ADVISORS

Early success is encouraging and exciting. However, it's like a drug; and there's danger if you don't balance the excitement with the strategy and skill required for getting the best results. This feeling of invincibility can cloud your judgment and cause you to ignore risks, which results in poor decision-making.

> THE FEELING OF INVINCIBILITY CAN CLOUD YOUR JUDGMENT AND CAUSE YOU TO IGNORE RISKS, WHICH RESULTS IN POOR DECISION-MAKING.

My great friend, client, and coauthor Peter Thomas has given this malady—the feeling of being invincible—a name: King Author's Disease. At first the victim feels as invincible as King Arthur; nothing can destroy him. He's drunk on the adrenaline of success. This disease is as dangerous to your career as it was to King Arthur, who rushed into battle without armor, against a foe he knew nothing about, because he had not done his research.

Ambitious individuals can get so caught up in the thrill of the chase that they overlook risks. They become overconfident and start to believe they're the smartest person in the room. They stop seeking advice from others, and that's when the challenges begin.

I went through an experience in my early twenties when I lost it all, and it taught me a valuable lesson: Don't operate in a vacuum, and don't let success go to your head. Get the best advisors you can obtain. Build a *Life Team* around you (see No. 39). Don't rely solely on your own judgment, because advisors can give you feedback you may not have thought of and insight you may not have seen. Reach out to mentors and other *Life Team* members who know your values and priorities.

There's another really valuable part of your *Life Team* when it comes to making wise decisions about all the challenges and considerations you face, and that's an informal board. Your board can consist of people who are already advising you—like mentors, family members, and trusted friends or colleagues. Running things by an informal board is a great way to thrash out any issues you face, either personally or professionally. I regularly send emails to my informal board to get their insight on ideas I might be considering.

This is one of the most powerful things you can do to prepare well for your life and business. Think about those around you whom you may already be going to for advice and counsel, and go ahead and set up your board. Then run things by them regularly before you make major decisions and see if that doesn't bring a new dimension to your success.

AMBITIOUS INDIVIDUALS CAN GET SO CAUGHT UP IN THE THRILL OF THE CHASE THAT THEY OVERLOOK RISKS. THEY BECOME OVERCONFIDENT AND START TO BELIEVE THEY'RE THE SMARTEST PERSON IN THE ROOM. THEY STOP SEEKING ADVICE FROM OTHERS, AND THAT'S WHEN THE CHALLENGES BEGIN.

41.
DO FAVORS IN ADVANCE (FIA)

When you help people win now, it creates wins for you in the future.

Favors in Advance are favors you do for people regardless of your status with them and without a desired outcome. You don't expect something in return; you just want to pay it forward and give value in advance. People like to do business with people who do things for them and who work to build a platform of trust. Why not be a giver?

I love to give things away. I keep books and other resources in the trunk of my car, and I carry them in my backpack for chance encounters, like in airplanes. In fact, I have a whole arsenal of giveaways, including helpful lists of websites, vendors, and even videos.

Do *Favors in Advance* and build a mental bank account of favors for your future. Have the right mindset; commit to loving, inspiring, and complimenting daily. Be generous, and help people win. (We'll have more on this later.)

> PEOPLE LIKE TO DO BUSINESS WITH PEOPLE WHO DO THINGS FOR THEM AND WHO WORK TO BUILD A PLATFORM OF TRUST.

42.
SURROUND YOURSELF WITH PEOPLE MORE SUCCESSFUL THAN YOURSELF

You become who you hang with. Because of the human need to be liked, your values and beliefs will slowly morph into those of the, say, five people you spend the most time around. Strategically select the people you hang with; consider whether the life they're living is one you want to live and whether they have the same values and beliefs you have.

It's impactful to surround yourself with people more successful than yourself in selected areas so you can learn from them. My protégé Ben Paige is twenty-three years old. The average age of the four or five people he spends the most time with is over sixty years old, and that's intentional on his part. Why? Because he knows hanging out with people who have the experience and wisdom he doesn't have in certain areas will make him smarter. He believes hanging around people who are more experienced will help him grow, which prepares him for a better future.

What I've said before bears repeating: *Advice Matters* (see my book of the same title). In fact, advice can be life changing. My life has certainly been enriched—and my success level has been highly impacted—by my coaches and mentors who have poured their knowledge and expertise into my life. We all have a choice about the people we spend time with. And with all the billions of people on this planet, life is simply too short not to invest your valuable time with those you can learn from and who motivate you to be your best.

If you don't have one or more mentors and/or a coach, get on it! Your future will be brighter!

> WE ALL HAVE A CHOICE ABOUT THE PEOPLE WE SPEND TIME WITH. AND WITH ALL THE BILLIONS OF PEOPLE ON THIS PLANET, LIFE IS SIMPLY TOO SHORT NOT TO INVEST YOUR VALUABLE TIME WITH THOSE YOU CAN LEARN FROM AND WHO MOTIVATE YOU TO BE YOUR BEST.

43.
BUILD YOUR OWN BRAND BY HELPING OTHERS WIN

My late friend, colleague, and mentor Zig Ziglar once said, "You can have everything in life you want if you will just help enough other people get what they want." I certainly believe that my lifestyle of helping others win prepared the way for the brand and business and life I'm blessed to enjoy today.

Your mental bank account in someone's eyes can grow or diminish. However, it's almost impossible to lose if you continually help other people win. Helping and serving others should be a way of life. Since we all have some narcissistic tendencies, many times we're are all about ourselves rather than looking for ways to help others. It's critical to understand that relationships work best when you look at how to help others win.

So many people get caught up in being right and appearing strong that they fail to understand the emotions that happen when they let other people win. For example, when someone shares a good idea, validate it! Use words like, "Tell me more" and let them win! When they win they feel good, their emotions go up, and you get more connected. Right? And when you get more connected, they get more behind your brand.

I'm constantly looking for ways the other person, the other company, the other client—anyone I want to influence—can win. Because of the research and the amount of study I've done on understanding people, I can often help people get clearer on what they actually want, and then help them get it. One of the best ways to help them get clarity is to understand what's on their map—their window. They see the world the way they see it because of their past ex-

> WHEN YOU'RE THINKING ABOUT OTHER PEOPLE AND NOT YOURSELF, YOU CAN HELP THEM BETTER UNDERSTAND WHAT THEY WANT AND HELP THEM GET IT.

periences—people they've spent time with, things they've done, things they've learned, and the good or bad things that have happened to them in life. When you're thinking about other people and not yourself, you can help them better understand what they want and help them get it. It's a win for them and a win for you as you prepare for your future because it enhances your brand. When you help someone win, you often create a fan for life.

[Callout:]

44.
EXPRESS GRATITUDE

When you express gratitude, your mindset is enhanced for living a more successful life. Be thankful by reflecting on the good things in your life, including your family, friends, your *Life Team,* and the people who do business with you.

Gratitude impacts the way you view life, and showing gratitude enriches your relationships in a huge way. How many thank-you cards have you sent in the last week? How many in the last month? How about in the last year? I send hundreds of cards every year, because I understand the power of appreciating people.

Gratitude makes you a better person and helps you be better mentally prepared for your future. There are many opportunities to dwell on the negative things that happen. You have to choose not to dwell on those, and decide instead to be grateful for all your blessings. That's what I focus on every day, and you should too. I prayerfully count my blessings each morning, and I balance contentment and enjoying what I have with constantly looking at my goals and aspirations and seeing where I want to go.

> GRATITUDE IMPACTS THE WAY YOU VIEW LIFE, AND SHOWING GRATITUDE ENRICHES YOUR RELATIONSHIPS IN A HUGE WAY.

Successful leaders regularly express gratitude for the positive things in their lives. Some even keep gratitude journals. When people realize you're grateful, they often want to keep giving. This obviously relates to both your personal and professional lives.

Authentic gratitude in business will go a long way. When you show people gratitude, it means you truly care about others and you recognize their gifts and talents—whether that's employees, colleagues, customers, and even managers, bosses, or a CEO above you. If you're not sure where to start, just begin by seeing and celebrating the positive in them.

It's also important to remember the people who make a difference in your life and show appreciation to them. Take a look back at the previous year and think about the people who touched your life along the way. Now take some time to list those individuals and ask yourself if they know how much you appreciate them. If they don't, what are you waiting for?

Aesop said, "Gratitude is the sign of noble souls." It is noble, indeed, to be thankful, as such a gesture shows humility and selflessness. When we step outside our sometimes-egocentric world to recognize that we cannot and do not control everything, we can acknowledge our day-to-day existence as a gift. Being grateful for whatever benefits we receive enables us to remember how fortunate and blessed we really are. This habit of expressing gratitude is also a fast track to a more positive outlook.

45.
GIVE BACK

Giving has so many angles of wins, including enhancing your own thinking so you're motivated to do more so you can give more.

Giving back can come in the form of time or money. Make an intentional effort to give back to those less fortunate than yourself, or even to those less knowledgeable than yourself. As you're going through life and you have experiences in certain areas, you can impact others by sharing the knowledge and wisdom you gained. When you give back to a group, a company, an organization, an individual, or even a family member, you're preparing them for the future and preparing yourself to be the best you can be.

> FIND SOMETHING YOU CAN BE PASSIONATE ABOUT AND GIVE BACK, EITHER PERSONALLY OR FINANCIALLY. IT WILL COME BACK TO YOU IN MORE WAYS THAN YOU EXPECT.

Find something you can be passionate about and give back, either personally or financially. It will come back to you in more ways than you expect.

46.
BE REAL

People appreciate transparency!

Real trumps perfectionism; and the more mentally prepared you are to be vulnerable, the bigger your impact. When the people around you know your heart, they'll realize that delivering value and being real are more important than being perfect. If you can muster up the self-esteem to be really real, your relationships go to another level. People appreciate it when you can tell them you've made a mistake and you're sorry. So many times people protect their egos and defend themselves at all costs. We all make mistakes—that's just the way God made the world. We're all imperfect and doing life, and being real matters.

> REAL TRUMPS PERFECTIONISM; AND THE MORE MENTALLY PREPARED YOU ARE TO BE VULNERABLE, THE BIGGER YOUR IMPACT.

Transparency isn't just about being honest with others; it's also about being honest and true to yourself. Are you living the life you want to live? If not, it can show. Stop for a moment to think about your life and about what you really want. What are you doing that you don't like to do? In preparing for your future, it's critically important that you're honest with yourself. You can only pretend to be happy for so long.

If you're living someone else's dream and not your own, it will show. Enthusiasm is contagious, and so is negativity and dissatisfaction. You can feel it when someone doesn't like what they do. People often get caught up in things they don't love or things out of their competency level. In order to be happy, successful, and authentic, it's best to know what you want and live it.

47.
BE A "CONNECTOR"

"Life is a series of presentations . . . make each one count."
−TONY JEARY

The more intentional you are about meeting, logging in, and helping connections, the more powerful you will be in life.

My dad kept stacks of business cards held together with rubber bands. When a friend or a customer asked about an issue, he would say, "No problem. Let me go to my business cards." He would know just where to go to pull out one of his thousands of cards and make a phone call to get a glass or a window fixed, or just about anything else anyone needed. I picked up the same habit of making those connections and surrounding myself with people to do life with.

At a young age I saw the power of being a connector by watching how my dad prepared. He collected information on people, and he built his own style of "Rolodex," if you will, of those who could help him. Then he used those same connections to help others. Today, when I have a particular result I'm looking for, it's a simple matter to call someone from my contact list who has the knowledge, expertise, or connections I need. The flip side of that, of course, is that I am always ready to help them win in any way I can. One way I do that is by constantly looking for ways to connect others, so I can make things happen and also bring value to other people as well as to myself.

While writing this part of the book, I'm in Fiji in one of those cool huts on the water. I had just had breakfast with the family when I got a text from a friend that said, "I have a friend who needs a wedding photographer. Would your daughter Paige be interested?" (See her web page at paigejearyphotogrpahy.org.) After a few texts back and forth, Paige is now connected, and perhaps a great win will happen. I love being a connector!

Are you a connector? Some people are more naturally gifted that way, and others may need to put thinking power into developing this trait. Just look for ways to create wins by connecting people with others who have the knowledge and expertise to help them get the results they want. They win and you win.

You can be even more valuable to your relationship database if you have a big arsenal and if you're more intentional about sharing it. Think of ways you can nurture your contacts. Send them notes, cards, and gifts of value. It doesn't have to be a large gift—it can be a book, an article, a video, or even a suggested URL. Connect others where it makes mutual sense for them, and you create automatic wins for yourself. It's a great way to pave the way for future success!

> LOOK FOR WAYS TO CREATE WINS BY CONNECTING PEOPLE WITH OTHERS WHO HAVE THE KNOWLEDGE AND EXPERTISE TO HELP THEM GET THE RESULTS THEY WANT. THEY WIN AND YOU WIN.

48.
BE A PERSON OF INFLUENCE

INFLUENCE IS THE ONE THING THAT MATTERS IN BUSINESS, ABOVE ALL ELSE. INFLUENCERS HAVE THE ABILITY TO CHANGE PEOPLE'S DECISIONS, GET PEOPLE TO BUY, AND CONVINCE OTHERS TO SEE THEIR POINT OF VIEW.

When you have a positive impact on people and create momentum and results, you have influence. When others know you as a person of action and rely on you to think alongside them, they trust that you have intellect, vision, and the ability to make things happen.

Influence is the one thing that matters in business, above all else. Influencers have the ability to change people's decisions, get people to buy, and convince others to see their point of view. People with influence have already built up an arsenal of respect, trust, credibility, and brand strength. People will gravitate toward them. Clients, colleagues, and prospects want to be a part of their world.

Since the ability to make things happen is a key trait of successful individuals, make sure you dedicate yourself early on to becoming a person of influence.

49.
FOCUS ON YOUR PEOPLE
OF INFLUENCE

You not only want to be a person of influence; you also want to focus on the *People of Influence* in your universe. POIs (*People of Influence*) are those who can have the most impact on your life and results, both personally and professionally. Your POIs may be customers or clients, they may be key team members, they may be a coach or a mentor, and they may be friends or family members.

Identify the top ten, fifteen, or twenty people who have the most influence over preparing you for success, and then take the time to understand what their priorities and goals are. That puts you in a position to nurture them and make sure they're winning; creating wins for them inevitably creates wins for you somewhere down the line. Keep in touch with them often, send them a card or gift on their birthday, and be sure to do *Favors in Advance*.

CREATING WINS FOR YOUR *PEOPLE OF INFLUENCE* INEVITABLY CREATES WINS FOR YOU SOMEWHERE DOWN THE LINE.

Knowing who your *People of Influence* are gives you a remarkable advantage as you prepare for your future. I want to encourage you to list your POIs in your phone, along with their goals and ambitions and how they want you to support them. That's being strategic, and it takes some effort. I coach my high achievers to do this, because it is such a huge piece of getting RESULTS faster!

50.
UNDERSTAND AND UTILIZE PERSONALITY PROFILING

Not everyone is like you. In fact, most people aren't. So how do you best prepare yourself to relate to the world around you?

Building relationships and working with different people requires an understanding of how people filter life through their own eyes. Most of us try to communicate with others the way we think, rather than through the way they think.

> UNDERSTANDING PERSONALITY STYLES WILL HELP YOU EXCEL AT BUSINESS, BECAUSE YOU CAN COMMUNICATE WITH PEOPLE IN THE WAY THEY WILL BEST UNDERSTAND.

Understanding personality styles will help you excel at business, because you can communicate with people in the way they will best understand. You may be into details, and yet you're presenting to a prospective buyer who only desires a high-level, fast overview. This person doesn't want all the details. By knowing your prospective buyer's personality style in advance, you can adapt your presentation to give a high-level view.

At TJI, we've carefully built a tool that produces a 52-page personality profile based on the DISC model to determine someone's personality. Here are the key points of the DISC personality profile:

- A "D" personality is a driver, a person who wants results. If you bore a D with details, you're certain to lose. D personalities will make buying decisions based on results and speed. If they determine you to be a slow, detailed, methodical thinker, it might work against you. If you perceive those traits as an asset, you'll miss the mark when it comes to communicating with your target.

- An "I" personality is an influencer, a person who likes to build relationships. They like to be social and participate in events where there is an opportunity to be people-centered. Often an I is persuasive and warm and able to build great alliances. They want people to support their ideas and opinions and get to know them. They want to be recognized.

- An "S" personality is steady and nurturing. They care about taking care of others and being very service-oriented. They want to talk feelings, not facts; they want approval. They don't like to be backed into a corner.

- A "C" personality is very compliant. They are analytical problem-solvers and detail-oriented. They like to perfect processes and work plans. Their high expectations of themselves and others can at times be critical. They want you to be sensitive of their time, and they want details. The more systematic and logical, the better for them.

Understand personality profiling and learn how to incorporate it into your life. (See our store at tonyjeary.com to order our profile tool.) It's important in both your personal life—with your spouse and kids—and in your professional life—with your bosses, employees, co-workers, and clients. By taking the time to learn the DISC language, you'll be much better prepared to communicate at the highest level.

51.
HIRE SUCCESSFUL, POSITIVE PEOPLE

Prepare smartly by hiring smart people. Obviously, some people are fast and some are slow, and some are smarter than others. Smart and fast is the best combination for future success, of course. With any other combination, things can happen that you'll have to undo.

> SMART AND FAST IS THE BEST COMBINATION FOR FUTURE SUCCESS. WITH ANY OTHER COMBINATION, THINGS CAN HAPPEN THAT YOU'LL HAVE TO UNDO.

A multiplier for smart and fast is a positive attitude, because attitude impacts culture. The right culture produces all kinds of wins.

As I've previously stated, having the right people around you is a big contributor to your success. As a leader, make sure you're prepared for success by replacing those who aren't right for you with those who are. Hire successful, positive people who can help you win better.

52.
BUILD RICH RELATIONSHIPS SO YOU'LL HAVE A RICH LIFE

Since I strongly believe that building solid relationships is one of the most important success strategies you can implement—both personally and professionally—I wrote a small book several years ago called *Rich Relationships, Rich Life*. I hope you will apply the truths below (mostly taken from the book) as you consider preparing well for life and success:

It's not about the grades you make as much as it is about the hands you shake.

This statement is not meant to insinuate that education and knowledge are not important – they are. What's even more important, though, for preparing to live the life you want is making connections and nurturing relationships. Strong relationships help you leverage your career growth, expand your success, create your legacy (both personally and professionally), and live a happier life.

> STRONG RELATIONSHIPS HELP YOU LEVERAGE YOUR CAREER GROWTH, EXPAND YOUR SUCCESS, CREATE YOUR LEGACY (BOTH PERSONALLY AND PROFESSIONALLY), AND LIVE A HAPPIER LIFE.

At the age of sixteen, I was introduced to the powerful book *How to Win Friends and Influence People* by Dale Carnegie, and it forever impacted my life for the better. Even before that book hit my hands, both my dad and my grandfather taught, demonstrated, and lived out how to live happy, to serve others, and to cultivate solid, life-long relationships. That's a strong legacy, and one that I'm blessed to have received.

Because I've intentionally chosen a career to serve others, coach the best, and be the strategist for many of the most successful organizations in the world, I decided to make my focus "Give value and do more than is expected." My organization (Tony Jeary International) thrives by this mantra. Every day we build more and deeper relationships by living it out. I propose that giving value as a focus will reap rewards beyond what you expect.

I believe there are three major components to getting the most out of the relationships in your life. You need to be:

1. **Strategic**. It has been my experience that being more strategic about what you want from each of the relationships in your life will set you up with a better chance for achieving what you want. Being strategic simply means that if you expect to get what you want, you need to be prepared to think about why you want it and how to go about getting the results you want—and for sure, create win/wins.

2. **Intentional**. In order for your relationships to really live up to their highest potential for you, you need to be intentional about them. Being intentional means scheduling time with each of the relationships that are important to you, knowing what's important to them, and ensuring you do those things. People will begin to notice that they are important to you when you are intentional, and they will want to reciprocate. Let people know they have value to you.

> ONE OF THE BEST WAYS TO HAVE RICH RELATIONSHIPS IS TO HELP OTHERS GET WHAT THEY WANT. IF YOU DON'T KNOW WHAT THEY WANT, ASK THEM!

3. **Disciplined** (about)
   - Building
   - Nourishing
   - Fostering

   Building, nourishing, and fostering positive relationships can make or break your happiness.

Here are seven things you can do to strategically and positively impact and grow your relationships:

1. **Ensure all stakeholders win.** Identify your stakeholders and look at how you can help each of them win.

2. **Understand what others want.** One of the best ways to have rich relationships is to help others get what they want. If you don't know what they want, ask them!

3. **Manage expectations.** To manage your own expectations, ask yourself, *Are they realistic?* It's okay and even advisable to have high expectations; it's just important to make sure your communication happens in a way that sets people up for success. To manage other people's expectations:

   - Start with knowing—ask people what their expectations are!

   - Communicate with clarity

   - Be flexible (solution-oriented)

4. **Do *Favors in Advance*** (see No. 41). Put yourself in a position to win by giving. (See our new book, *Strategic Gifting.*) When I meet someone new, I often send them a gift. And for the last several years I've had an annual networking party to encourage connections and wins among my close contacts. I also do favors at those parties—I connect people, I give gifts, and I do my best to send each person home happy they attended.

   > PUT YOURSELF IN A POSITION TO WIN BY GIVING.

5. **Leverage personality styles** (see No. 50).

6. **Identify your *People of Influence*** (see No. 49).

7. **Have a partnership mentality.** If the person you're doing business with thinks like you do and truly wants a win/win, start immediately reframing your perspective from a "vendor/client" mentality to a true "partnership mentality." Then take mental ownership of your client's vision, considering how you can help that person or organization win and how you can succeed.

Remember as you prepare for life that the more intentional you are about establishing rich relationships, the more fulfilling your life will be.

53.
LISTEN UP!

In business and in life, listening is a critical skill. People who don't listen well often miss key indicators, clues, and components that drive relationships as well as important opportunities. Listening well is the key to excellent decision making and can make the difference between success and failure.

In my new book *Introduction to NLP* (Neuro-Linguistic Programming), I list five steps that lead to the most effective listening, because they show the person you are engaged and genuinely interested in what they're saying. These five techniques lead to quick and strong rapport:

> LISTENING WELL IS THE KEY TO EXCELLENT DECISION MAKING AND CAN MAKE THE DIFFERENCE BETWEEN SUCCESS AND FAILURE.

1. Mentally repeat
2. Show listening
3. Encourage with sounds
4. Repeat back for accuracy
5. Review within the first eight hours

And here's another one: In his book *How to Win Friends and Influence People,* Dale Carnegie lists as his seventh principle, "Be a good listener. Encourage others to talk about themselves." A couple of years ago I met my new friends Rob and Jennifer Flick at an airport in New York. They were on their way back from Russia; and Rob had actually been sitting in the airport reading my book RESULTS Faster! when they recognized me from my picture on the cover and came over to ask me to autograph his book. I was intentional about asking them to tell me about themselves, and I listened! We ended up connecting in an instant friendship, which eventually evolved into a powerfully successful business partnership!

When someone in my audience or in a strategy session says something interesting and I want to go deeper, I'll often say "Tell me more," and then I listen. As a strategist, I talk 20 percent of the time and listen the other 80 percent. People love to talk about themselves, and sometimes the fastest way to win someone over is to simply listen, rather than talking and giving your opinion.

> "BE A GOOD LISTENER. ENCOURAGE OTHERS TO TALK ABOUT THEMSELVES."
> —DALE CARNEGIE

In my private RESULTS Studio we have a unique way of letting our clients know we're listening. In fact, the entire studio session is built around listening. We project the client information and ideas onto a screen for everyone to see, and we have an assistant who takes notes and catalogs the ideas offered up in the room throughout the day. And yet we go much deeper than just note-taking. We have a specific proprietary matrix document that contains the name of every individual in the room. During the meeting, we ask each person to contribute, and we write what they say on the matrix document. Then at the end of each session, we go around the room and ask each individual to give us their main takeaway for the day and tell us whether they perceived our process to be valuable for them. That way we actually get their live feedback before they leave. It's a very good process for strengthening the bond with the client and for building credibility.

Listening involves both concentration and contribution. You must concentrate to actually hear the point the person is conveying and to block out distracting thoughts; and you must use discipline to refrain from speaking when you have something to say. Contribution should only come after the person talking has adequately communicated their ideas.

Are you a good listener? If you want to prepare well for life and success, you should be.

54.
MAKE OTHERS FEEL SIGNIFICANT

There's a difference between appreciating people and making them feel significant. Of course, you want to appreciate others. Even more than that, though, you need to make those important people in your life feel significant.

Success typically comes in your life (both personally and professionally) with the help of others who fill gaps for you and who are your cheerleaders and top supporters. There is rarely an exception to this. Think of those people in your own life. Do you make those people feel like they're significant? Do you brag on them in the presence of others? Do you give others credit? Do you ask for other people's opinions on things important to you and to the success of your company? Are you interested in the things that matter to them?

What are you doing to make your clients feel special and significant? I have a standard I call the "black-card" standard. Achieving *Black-Card Level* is the most elite level, and it comes with special treatment. This is what we want to be known for—giving others the black-card treatment. When clients fly in to meet with me, we pick them up in our customized Sprinter RESULTS1 van and provide a luxurious drive to my private RESULTS Studio. We offer our many resources at no extra charge, we create a spa-like atmosphere in the restroom, we have an outside lounge where people can gather at break times, we offer up healthy snacks and drinks, and we even sometimes wash their vehicles if they've driven themselves. We want our clients to feel like we are their concierge service and that all the details matter—that they matter.

> MAKE PEOPLE FEEL SIGNIFICANT. PEOPLE BLOSSOM UNDER APPROVAL, COMPLIMENTS, AND FEELING LOVED.

How do you think it would affect your future if you did the same for people who are special in your life? Make people feel significant. People blossom under approval, compliments, and feeling loved.

55.
PROVIDE JOY AND ENTERTAINMENT

Early on, I studied the distinctions that make certain speakers more in demand than others, and I found three primary reasons why speakers are hired: 1) they can bring great value, 2) they have a big name and can bring celebrity appeal, or 3) they bring entertainment and the smile factor. I've discovered over the years that people actually learn more when they're happy and being entertained.

PEOPLE ACTUALLY LEARN MORE WHEN THEY'RE HAPPY AND BEING ENTERTAINED.

People really do like to be entertained, whether you're making formal presentations, conducting meetings, or just living life. I asked my wife once why she married me, and she said, "One reason is because you're entertaining." My kids love for me to put smiles on their faces as well! And my clients tell me they really enjoy the fun factor I bring in my sessions/presentations. I hand out dollar bills and encourage laughter and fun throughout.

Do you know that laughter is one of the best things you can do for your body? When you make people laugh, you're helping them reduce stress and actually changing the atmosphere of the room. People forget about their negative feelings, and they connect better with others in the room.

Wouldn't you like to have a brand where people say, "You know, I really want to be around those people because they bring joy and happiness"? Discovering how you can bring joy and entertainment to other people's lives is a great way to bring meaning to your own life. What can you do to be entertaining, and how can you help other people have more joy? Learn to laugh, have fun, be entertaining, and bring a cheerful heart to as many people as you can. When you provide joy and entertainment, you'll attract more of it!

VII. COMMUNICATION

Life truly is a series of presentations.
—TONY JEARY

The way we communicate with others and with ourselves
ultimately determines the quality of our lives.
—ANTHONY ROBBINS

Take advantage of every opportunity to practice your
communication skills so that when important occasions
arise, you will have the gift, the style, the sharpness,
the clarity, and the emotions to affect other people.
—JIM ROHN

56.
HAVE GREAT MEETINGS

The number one answer that most HR professionals give when they're asked what would best improve their organization's culture is "communication." And in my opinion, the number one issue within communication is meetings. Why? When you have great meetings with clear objectives, clear preparation, and an aligned agenda, you insure less time spent in meetings (hence, freeing up hours a week for focusing on HLAs) and you have better meeting outcomes!

WHEN YOU HAVE GREAT MEETINGS WITH CLEAR OBJECTIVES, CLEAR PREPARATION, AND AN ALIGNED AGENDA, YOU INSURE LESS TIME SPENT IN MEETINGS (HENCE, FREEING UP HOURS A WEEK FOR FOCUSING ON HLAS) AND YOU HAVE BETTER MEETING OUTCOMES!

I believe meetings are the cornerstone of communication inside a company. That's why I teach people all over the world how to have better meetings. As I've taught, trained, and written books about effective meetings for over twenty years, I've come to realize that meeting effectiveness is divided into three parts: preparation, delivery, and follow up. And when I ask people about their meeting effectiveness, the piece they're missing most often is preparation.

How about you? Do you have a good system for preparing for meetings? You should. One of the big pieces to the preparation puzzle is getting clear on your objectives. People often make the mistake of going straight into the agenda before they talk about the objectives. It's important to understand that *objectives trump the agenda.*

Another big piece is preparing well before you get to the meeting—doing things like strategically thinking through the invitation you send and who to invite, as well as determining the pre-work or pre-reads you need to do so you can be fully updated. Sometimes that means you'll need to do selected research or gathering of data so you can bring the right things to the table to make your meeting as effective as it can be.

To find out more about preparing well for meetings, see my book *We've Got to Start Meeting and Emailing Like This.*

57.
REHEARSING HELPS TAKE YOU FROM THE UNKNOWN TO THE KNOWN

The book I wrote years ago, *Nervous to Natural*, has helped thousands of people reach and even exceed their communication goals by helping them achieve confidence. Everyone wants to be more confident in certain ways when they're communicating, and one of the basic premises of the book is that you can do that by simply taking the unknown to the known.

When you're preparing for a presentation, one of the best ways to take the unknown to the known is by rehearsing. One day years ago I walked into my media room and found my ten-year-old daughter rehearsing for a presentation she was going to make at school the next day. She had all her dolls set out on chairs, and she was using them as her audience. I had to get a picture!

Your rehearsal doesn't have to be formal; it could be more like role-playing. I had a client in yesterday who was on his way with his team to meet with the owner of one of his client companies. I had given them targeted bullet points and suggested that they rehearse them in my van on the way to their meeting. He sent me a note this morning saying the client had given them everything they asked for. I love success stories!

WHEN YOU'RE PREPARING FOR A PRESENTATION, ONE OF THE BEST WAYS TO TAKE THE UNKNOWN TO THE KNOWN IS BY REHEARSING.

58.
BE READY FOR TOUGH QUESTIONS

We had another client company over this morning, and I was talking to them about a subject I've written twenty-six books about—presentation effectiveness. I was sharing with them that most people prepare just by rehearsing, because they think of presentation as just a skill. Even though rehearsal is powerful, being strategic about your presentation effectiveness goes beyond that. It includes utilizing tools, processes, and technology.

One sure way to be more effective is to prepare ahead by thinking through what the tough questions will be. In my book *RESULTS Faster!* I said you have to be an extraordinary persuader if you want to be an extraordinary leader, and I listed twelve principles for effective persuasion. The last one was to "preempt objections." No matter who you're trying to persuade, prepare ahead by determining what the tough questions may be, what the best answers are, and who's best to answer them.

NO MATTER WHO YOU'RE TRYING TO PERSUADE, PREPARE AHEAD BY DETERMINING WHAT THE TOUGH QUESTIONS MAY BE, WHAT THE BEST ANSWERS ARE, AND WHO'S BEST TO ANSWER THEM.

Just before I wrote *RESULTS Faster!* I was working with the president of a large organization who was getting ready to do a group presentation about his company to a specific group of analysts. I thought the analysts would probably have objections to his vision (and they did), and I knew he needed to be ready. We had pre-prepared responses, and he and his team were able to communicate the fundamentals back to their audience. This session was being recorded and was going all over the world, and he had a big win because he was prepared and ready with the answers to those objections ahead of time. We all should do this—be ready!

So this morning I created a matrix for my clients and had them list the eight or ten toughest questions they could come up with about their business. Their homework assignment was to research the best answers to those questions inside their own organization, summarize them, and then go out and train everyone on them. That way, they would have the best of the best answers to the toughest questions going out to their entire team. To me, that's being fully prepped and ready to have an impact.

59.
PLAN CASCADING

Before you start a meeting or a presentation, think about what follow-up activities need to happen.

Cascading—communicating something important to another level of people, either inside or outside your organization—sometimes needs to go several layers deep. At the time I was coaching the president of Walmart, the company had 2.1 million employees. That meant when he and I developed a communication, it had to be cascaded down fifteen levels; so he had to think about how it could be cascaded consistently down through that many levels throughout their 4,000 stores (just in the US alone).

The big answer in that kind of situation is to make sure you're thinking about cascading *before* your meetings or whatever you're doing, and then make sure you develop tools so everyone can use the same ones. You're more prepared to cascade if you build a shell of a tool—like a PowerPoint, a matrix, a handout, or even a video—and then fill in that shell as the information comes together. If everyone is using that same tool, the consistency is obviously so much better.

Many people miss strategic cascading altogether, most fail to do it, and even fewer plan from the start who needs to get what information and develop the tools to do it (i.e., notes to share for speed and consistency).

> MAKE SURE YOU'RE THINKING ABOUT CASCADING BEFORE YOUR MEETINGS OR WHATEVER YOU'RE DOING, AND THEN MAKE SURE YOU DEVELOP TOOLS SO EVERYONE CAN USE THE SAME ONES.

60.
Study Presentation Mastery™ As a Strategic Asset

Build your presentation effectiveness so you're prepared for any and all communications. As we mentioned earlier, some people think about presentation effectiveness as just a skill. Skill is certainly important. However, I believe that *Presentation Mastery*™ is much more than that; it's an asset, to both individuals and companies alike.

In 2003 we published with Simon & Schuster a book I authored called *Life Is a Series of Presentations*. Think about it: Every encounter you have—whether it's with a colleague, a friend, a customer, or your spouse— you're presenting yourself. And you're representing yourself and/or your business. The way you present your thoughts and ideas to people really does make a difference, whether it's to someone waiting in line at a grocery store or to someone you just met. Your presentation can have a profound impact and shape someone's life, or it can be the key to whether someone takes action on your behalf.

> IF WE WANT TO MASTER THE HUNDREDS OF PRESENTATIONS WE MAKE EACH WEEK, WE NEED TO BE PROFICIENT IN THREE AREAS: THE PREPARATION, THE DELIVERY, AND THE FOLLOW UP.

The essence of the book is that if we want to master the hundreds of presentations we make each week, we need to be proficient in three areas: the preparation, the delivery, and the follow up. So ask yourself, *How do I prepare better? How do I prepare to deliver better?* And then, *How do I prepare to follow up?*

This morning I was on a phone call with a client in New York, and one of the team members wanted me to prepare a letter for one of their clients to help them understand their value prop. As a presentation master I was prepared enough to say, "Why don't we talk about it while we're on the phone, and we'll write what I think you want on the screen; then we can adjust it as needed, and we'll have it ready to send right to you." So I went over the situation, the need, and the value of what they bring to the table, as well as the outcome they want and the deliverables. After we had summarized all that on the screen, we were able to prepare the entire letter right then. Within just a few minutes I was able to send it to her so she could forward it on.

Presentations masters understand that they need to think through all the little nuances and be prepared with *Planned Spontaneity* (see No. 33) to get the best results. Preparation is really being aware of all the different possibilities.

61.
ASK QUESTIONS TO GET LEVERAGE

The more you know, the smarter you are and the better decisions you make—hence, the better the results you get.

Many years ago, when I started hanging around my wife's family quite a bit before we were married, her grandfather made a comment to her and her parents: "Man, that kid asks a lot of questions!" They explained to him that I asked all those questions because I really wanted to understand the family and be prepared to become a contributing member. I believe he eventually grew to respect me for that, because I came to understand their priorities and held the same Christian beliefs they had. In effect, my asking so many questions prepared me to launch more successfully into the family. Of course, I have encouraged my girls to do the same.

> THE MORE YOU KNOW, THE SMARTER YOU ARE AND THE BETTER DECISIONS YOU MAKE— HENCE, THE BETTER THE RESULTS YOU GET.

That's just one example of the value of asking questions so you can get answers that will help you be more prepared. Here's how we capitalize on that in our office: Maritza, one of my strong, energetic team members, has developed a great system to help me prepare for meetings, phone calls, and events. Sometimes that involves putting a *Smart Report* in front of me based on research she's done; sometimes it's printing out handouts that I can study; and sometimes it's getting notes from past meetings in front of me. All those things allow me to ask myself questions like *What did we do in the last connection? Where do we need to go from here? How can I help the most? What is their world right now?* Then I can leverage the answers to all those questions and be more prepared for whatever I'm doing, including making decisions on any issues that come up.

And here's another valuable bonus you could get from asking questions: connection with your kids. Over the years, I have intentionally and carefully asked questions and listened to my kids. I want to sincerely know their world, their thinking, and ways I might guide and support them. My daughter Brooke says to me from time to time, "Dad, I love it that you listen to me." If you're not doing that with your kids (or not doing it to the level you could), maybe that's a habit you need to pick up.

VIII. BEING READY

As a rule, we find what we look for; we achieve what we get ready for.
—JAMES CASH PENNY

It is not often that a man can make opportunities for himself.
But he can put himself in such shape that when or
if the opportunities come, he is ready.
—THEODORE ROOSEVELT

In any situation, there is always someone who's the most prepared.
Decide now that you're going to be that person, and make it
part of your brand. A mindset that says, I will always prep
and be ready ahead of time is simply a philosophy that sparks success.
—TONY JEARY

62.
CONFIDENCE COMES FROM BEING READY

Being ready comes from intentionality—purposefully thinking ahead to what you can do now to position yourself to be the best, the top, the winner—and confidence comes from being ready.

Confidence can be an opportunity magnet. Many people are attracted to someone who is confident and has vision. I think people can often sense when you're excited about sharing something because you've really prepared and you're ready—you've done your homework and you're ready to answer any tough questions. You're able to convert that energy and inspiration into confidence, and you deliver well. You're not worried about perfectionism; you're more focused on sharing what you're doing, and your confidence just keeps going up.

> BEING READY COMES FROM INTENTIONALITY— PURPOSEFULLY THINKING AHEAD TO WHAT YOU CAN DO NOW TO POSITION YOURSELF TO BE THE BEST, THE TOP, THE WINNER—AND CONFIDENCE COMES FROM BEING READY.

Part of that confidence comes from mental ownership. As I encouraged you to do in the introduction, create a mindset that says, *I will always prep and be ready ahead of time.* Decide now that you're going to be the person who is the most prepared in any situation, and make it part of your brand.

As I've traveled the world working in over fifty countries over a period of now thirty-plus years (wow!), I've never been a minute late to a gig. I've always been there, and early. My mental commitment is that I'm going to be the most prepared and ready. How about yours?

63.
ORGANIZE EVERY DAY

Be consistently organized, so you're ready for future opportunities at all levels. If you fail to organize, then you often miss out—you don't have the proper amount of time, you lose things, and you don't operate at peak performance.

In our company, we have ten performance standards that we operate by every day. When I was developing those standards, I thought through them very carefully and have, of course, refined them over the years. Item number three on the list is to keep everything organized at all times, because we believe when you're super organized, you're really prepared for just about anything that can happen. We have the standards posted in every room, and I also have my team include them in the very first in-person interview when they're recruiting someone for our firm.

> ORGANIZE EVERY DAY IN EVERY WAY, SO YOU CAN TAKE ADVANTAGE OF OPPORTUNITIES, YOU CAN SAVE TIME, YOU'RE LESS STRESSED, AND YOU CAN OPERATE AT YOUR VERY BEST.

I do a ton of coaching in the medical field, where I teach doctors and dentists (and their teams) how to be more efficient. One of the things I teach them is to be so organized that they can close their eyes and reach over to any drawer in any of their rooms and know what's in that drawer so they can pull out the tool they need. Most of them are quite intrigued that I go into that much detail with the concept of organization. And yet going to that level yields so many benefits—like *saving time,* impressing their patients, avoiding frustration, and really being in their game.

I encourage you to organize every day in every way, so you can take advantage of opportunities, you can save time, you're less stressed, and you can operate at your very best.

64.
Have Backup for Everything

Having backup for everything ensures you're ahead of the game instead of scrambling when something unforeseen happens. That could include:

- Not just gathering the necessary equipment and tools, but also having extra on hand—pins for signing, flashlights, toothbrush, batteries etc.

- Organizing your computer and insuring it's ready to perform—with a backup battery, backed up software, backup information, a backup list of codes, etc. A computer is a wonderful resource and performs as a supercharger as long as it's always organized, loaded, and ready to perform.

THINGS GO OUT AND THINGS BREAK, AND WHEN YOU HAVE BACKUP... WELL, YOU HAVE INSURANCE.

I'm constantly thinking about (and teaching others to think about) all the what-ifs that can happen in life. For example, we usually have two printers in every room; so if one printer goes out, we can just keep going because we have a backup. We have extra paper, extra ink, extra pens, etc. In fact, I even keep an extra LED projector in my RESULTS1 van and a backup computer and batteries in two of my vehicles. I keep extra everything in all categories, everywhere I can. Things go out and things break, and when you have backup... well, you have insurance.

65.
PLAN FOR WHAT-IFS IN YOUR MEETINGS

By thinking ahead, you can be ready to take action when what-ifs happen in your meetings.

In our *Presentation Mastery*™ system that I developed and teach, I encourage people to not only be aware of their tough questions and know how to answer them, but to also to be aware of the what-ifs. For example, think ahead about what you would do if someone shows up late to a meeting or if someone leaves a meeting early. Have a backup summary document, so when someone needs to leave early, you can hand it to them and they'll have the summary of what they're missing. Or if someone shows up a third of the way into the meeting, you can hand them a briefing document they can read over and catch up with everyone else. And be sure to have extra handouts available in case more people show up for the meeting than you expected.

> THINKING ABOUT AND TAKING PRECAUTIONS FOR THE WHAT-IFS IN ADVANCE IS A LEVEL OF PREPAREDNESS THAT EVERYONE SHOULD ASPIRE TO HAVE.

Thinking about and taking precautions for the what-ifs in advance can be very powerful and impressive. It's a level of preparedness that everyone should aspire to have.

66.
BE DEPENDENT ON GOD

I encourage you to pray a lot.

In order to be ready for the day—every day—breathe deeply and pray first thing in the morning. Make this a personal standard, as I do.

Prayer is actually the best preparation tool you can have. The Bible tells us to pray and trust God. We need to really think about how we start our day. Are we praying that we will be in God's will? I do that every morning, and often throughout the day before I start working on a project. When we do that, He will help us do things and see things through His perspective.

> PRAYER IS ACTUALLY THE BEST PREPARATION TOOL YOU CAN HAVE.

When you're praying, make sure you're able to hear God speak back to you. Pray for discernment and that you'll really be able to receive what He has to say. Pray that you'll be ready to share, support, give, and love as He directs. And be sure to create flexibility in your schedule to make time for any divine appointments He may send your way so you can bless someone—or so someone can bless you.

> BE SURE TO CREATE FLEXIBILITY IN YOUR SCHEDULE TO MAKE TIME FOR ANY DIVINE APPOINTMENTS HE MAY SEND YOUR WAY SO YOU CAN BLESS SOMEONE—OR SO SOMEONE CAN BLESS YOU.

67.
ESTABLISH RULES BEFORE YOU START THE GAME

By preparing guidelines and practical rules of engagement, you can better manage expectations and enjoy a smoother ride. Unmet or unrealistic expectations can kill success, so establish them up front and make sure everyone buys in.

For example, before I make a phone call, I will often think about what the objective is, or the action I want to happen. Then as soon as I start the call, I'll frame it by saying, "Hey, Bob, I was thinking our call would be about (this subject), and we'll see if we can (accomplish this objective). And I think we could probably do it in fifteen minutes or less. Is that your thinking?" And Bob would probably say, "Yes, that would be great!" So what I just did was establish the objective and the time frame. Then I might say, "From a rules standpoint, let's check it out fifteen minutes from now; if we've accomplished our objective, then we're done. If we need a little more time, let's renegotiate and maybe go twenty minutes. Is that all right with you?"

> BY PREPARING GUIDELINES AND PRACTICAL RULES OF ENGAGEMENT, YOU CAN BETTER MANAGE EXPECTATIONS AND ENJOY A SMOOTHER RIDE. UNMET OR UNREALISTIC EXPECTATIONS CAN KILL SUCCESS, SO ESTABLISH THEM UP FRONT AND MAKE SURE EVERYONE BUYS IN.

The phone call is just one example. The same can apply to any meeting or presentation. Just list the objectives at the beginning, establish the time frame, and communicate your rules of engagement. Then get buy-in from your audience. The bottom line is, when you foreshadow the objectives and establish the rules at the start, you've set the expectations in motion and you'll be able to accomplish more in less time.

68.
BENCHMARK FOR BEST PRACTICES

Are you open-minded and prepared to improve? High achievers want to grow and expand as professionals, while also taking their team and organization to high levels of results. Benchmarking is a powerful way to bring best practices to your organization.

Several years ago I wrote a little book called *Leadership 25*, which is an assessment tool strategically designed for top leaders. Item number four of the assessment is benchmarking—looking at best practices and modeling part or all of them to grow your effectiveness. How well do you benchmark yourself, your organization, and your team? Do you benchmark the best attributes of your competition?

> HIGH ACHIEVERS WANT TO GROW AND EXPAND AS PROFESSIONALS, WHILE ALSO TAKING THEIR TEAM AND ORGANIZATION TO HIGH LEVELS OF RESULTS. BENCHMARKING IS A POWERFUL WAY TO BRING BEST PRACTICES TO YOUR ORGANIZATION.

People often get a little embarrassed because they don't really benchmark like they should. If that includes you, here's an "aha" that may help you: Why don't you designate someone on your team to be that fully devoted, proactive person who is constantly looking at the best practices and serving them up to you and your team? Then you'll have an ongoing, built-in benchmarking mechanism, versus just doing a one-off from time to time. It's a great way to get the best results for your organization!

69.
BE "PRESENTATION READY"

"Presentation ready" is a concept I coined years ago, which is a state of mind where you're constantly thinking and preparing ahead. For example, if your boss, board, or partners call and say they need a report on something, you're not stressed because you've already been gathering information; and with just a little touchup, you're ready. Or if a client calls and asks about billing or something you've talked about, you've been so good at taking notes and keeping them in a file that you can pull them right up and send them out to them. Or if an unexpected meeting comes up, you can pull things from your arsenal.

> IF YOU WANT TO OPERATE WITH PRESENTATION READINESS, BE SURE TO CREATE SYSTEMS SO YOU HAVE INFORMATION READY WHEN NEEDED, AND MAKE SURE IT CAN BE RETRIEVED QUICKLY.

Being *Presentation Ready* (see my book *Inspire Any Audience*) can often make or break an opportunity. If you want to operate with presentation readiness, be sure to create systems so you have information ready when needed, and make sure it can be retrieved quickly.

70.
DEVELOP PERSEVERANCE

One of the traits of high achievers is the ability to keep going, over and over again, no matter what obstacles they face. Perseverance is not optional.

Forbes magazine published a study in September 2013 called "The Six Disciplines Entrepreneurs Need to Succeed." One of those disciplines was mental toughness. If you're resilient, you will be able to bounce back from the setbacks you *will* face. Some will be small, and others will seem overwhelming. You must cultivate mental toughness and the determination to press on despite obstacles if you're going to survive and thrive in the business world.

Here's what will win in the end: simply being willing to keep going, switch gears, attempt new things, and work harder than others are willing to work. Having an attitude of perseverance will keep you focused on the end goal and keep you solution-oriented.

I've had major setbacks in my own life. I became a millionaire before I was twenty-five, and then I lost everything when the market changed suddenly. However, I bounced back by having an attitude of perseverance with a determination to make something positive out of my traumatic experiences.

WHEN YOU DEVELOP PERSEVERANCE, YOU'LL BE READY TO BREAK THROUGH ANY SETBACKS THAT COME YOUR WAY.

John Quincy Adams once said, "Patience and perseverance have a magical effect, before which difficulties disappear and obstacles vanish." When you develop perseverance, you'll be ready to break through any setbacks that come your way.

IX. INVESTING FOR YOUR FUTURE

An investment in knowledge pays the best interest.
—BENJAMIN FRANKLIN

The best investment you can make is in yourself.
—WARREN BUFFETT

A dream is your creative vision for your life in the future.
You must break out of your current comfort zone and become
comfortable with the unfamiliar and the unknown.
—DENIS WAITLEY

Invest in yourself now and reap the dividends
day after day after month after year.
—JACK LALANNE

71.
UNCOVER YOUR *BLIND SPOTS*

Everyone has *Blind Spots*—things on your *Belief Window* that you can't see unless uncovered by something or someone else. In order to move through life *better*, you need to get advice that will help you uncover your *Blind Spots* and change your *Belief Window*. Invest the time to uncover them now, and you can often save even more time later.

If there's an area in your life where you're not getting the results you want, it's very likely you have a *Blind Spot* (or many) that's getting in your way. Let me give you four very effective ways to identify *Blind Spots:*

1. Actively look for any beliefs that might be sabotaging you.

2. If you're experiencing stress about something, there's probably a belief getting in your way—look to see what the belief is.

3. Check your beliefs to make sure they're up to date. Are you using a year 2010 "operating system" to try and run your 2019 life?

4. Get advice. Ask someone you trust (a mentor, coach, or colleague) to help you figure out your *Blind Spots*.

One of the best things you can do to invest in your future success

IN ORDER TO MOVE THROUGH LIFE BETTER, YOU NEED TO GET ADVICE THAT WILL HELP YOU UNCOVER YOUR *BLIND SPOTS* AND CHANGE YOUR *BELIEF WINDOW.*

is to make sure you have the right kind of people around you to give you right kind of input—people who have reached the kind of success you aspire to and people who have been where you are. These seasoned people are often older and for sure have more life experience. They may be able to see things you can't see and help you choose a smarter path versus continuing down the wrong road.

Whatever your *Blind Spots* are, they are probably keeping you from being the best you can be. Inaccurate principles, missed distinctions, and overlooked perspectives hinder your results.

72.
ENSURE A POWERFUL PERSONAL BRAND IN THE FUTURE

Having a strong brand makes a big impact on your future. What are you known for? What is your top strength? Most people don't strategically develop their brands; they just let their reputations play themselves out.

I suggest you be strategic about building your personal brand. A successful brand represents who you are; it's your unique promise. Build a brand based not only on what you want to be and how you want to live, but also who you actually are and the core of how you live today. People want to do things with people they trust and respect. They want to know you will get the job done. They want to know you bring value to their world.

> A SUCCESSFUL BRAND REPRESENTS WHO YOU ARE. IT'S YOUR UNIQUE PROMISE. PEOPLE WANT TO DO THINGS WITH PEOPLE THEY TRUST AND RESPECT.

The bottom line is this: We all have a brand. Top leaders are strategic about building theirs. Think about your brand and determine how you want to be known. Then build it out and leverage it every way you can.

If you have a great brand, people want to be around you. If you're a happy person, a person who gets things done, and a person who wants the best out of others, those qualities are attractive to most people. I encourage you to think about what you can do to be more impactful to people you meet or those in your circle of influence. Certainly, things like doing favors, sharing, giving, and serving now ensure a powerful personal brand in the future. What we give to others comes back to us tenfold.

Here are some other things to think about when you're building your brand:

1. **Brand description**. I encourage you to write down four to six

characteristics that describe you and/or that you'd like to be described by.

2. **What people are missing about you.** Write down any distinctions that people don't really know about, or maybe that people misunderstand about you. You need to determine how to make these characteristics part of the brand you want to have.

3. **Uniqueness.** Write down three or four qualities that truly make you special. Maybe it's your history. You may have been with a company for a long time, and you have an exceptional understanding of a certain process, or maybe you have a long history in one particular niche and you're extremely gifted in that particular area.

4. **What people think of you.** Write down three or four words that describe your perception of how people perceive you.

5. **Attributes prized in the workplace (or at home).** Write down the attributes or qualities you possess that are valued in your organization (or in your home), and include the attributes and qualities you want to be valued for. Who you want to become is important.

6. **Your core value proposition.** What are the core characteristics that are valuable to your effectiveness? I am an encourager, and that is the core characteristic that makes me valuable to my clients. So my core value proposition would be, "I encourage people. I want to support them and bring out the best in them. I am constantly looking at ways to bring more value." Write down the core value proposition you bring to the world.

73.
Develop a Memorable, Influential Persona

Going beyond building your brand, here's one more thing to think about: Are you memorable?

What specifically do you want people to remember about you? And I'm not just talking about your personality; you don't have to have the most dynamic personality to be memorable. It has more to do with your presence—a certain image that causes people to see you as a particular kind of person. Your trademark expression, style, or persona makes you memorable... or not. Maybe you're humorous, carefree, or extremely positive, and people remember you for that. Or maybe you stand out because you do an extraordinary job of making a difference in the lives of others. People remember those who impact their lives.

> YOUR TRADEMARK EXPRESSION, STYLE, OR PERSONA MAKES YOU MEMORABLE... OR NOT.

Since most everyone loves to talk about themselves, one way to make an immediate impact is to ask them something about their life. When they respond, say, "Tell me more!" And then be genuinely interested in their reply. No one likes to be ignored. Yet we live in a society where everyone is ignoring everyone else in favor of texting, emailing, and talking about themselves. How many times have you been engaged in a conversation with someone new, and you could tell they weren't really listening as you were talking; they were simply waiting for their turn to talk? We have all been guilty of meeting someone new and instantly forgetting their name. How you approach others and paying attention to detail when directly interfacing with them will impact how others view you. You could be different and more memorable by intentionally focusing better on other people.

Is this an area you could possibly improve in? Most of us can. Ask yourself, *Am I genuinely interested in people, to the point that I'm building a positive strategic presence that significantly affects my results?* If this

WHATEVER MAKES YOU MEMORABLE AND AUTHENTICALLY YOU, EMBRACE IT AND BRING IT OUT IN EVERYTHING YOU DO.

is an area that needs work, start asking questions and being genuinely interested in others.

Whatever makes you memorable and authentically you, embrace it and bring it out in everything you do.

74.
WORK ON YOUR BODY LANGUAGE AND APPEARANCE

Most high achievers understand that it's important to be presentable. After all, you are your business; and when potential clients meet you, they'll judge you and your success by the things they see within the first few seconds, as well as whether partnering with you would bring them success. It doesn't matter if it's your car, your office, or your clothes. People will form an opinion of you by what they see.

Part of building your brand is being strategic about the way you look. This is beyond vanity; it's about excellence. Each day you make choices: *Do I want to be excellent today? Do I want to think, communicate, and convey a strong, authentic, and positive image?* Like it or not, people judge you on the way you look, think, and communicate. A smile makes people perceive you as approachable. A scowl, or ignoring people while you text, sends a different message. Truth is, most people build a reputation based on who they are, what they've done, and/or how they look, and yet they're not intentional about it.

> WHEN POTENTIAL CLIENTS MEET YOU, THEY'LL JUDGE YOU AND YOUR SUCCESS BY THE THINGS THEY SEE WITHIN THE FIRST FEW SECONDS, AS WELL AS WHETHER PARTNERING WITH YOU WOULD BRING THEM SUCCESS.

The more clarity you have on your brand, the more intentional you can be about the way you look. Are you doing your best to convey the best impression? Be wardrobe appropriate, use open body language, and send the message that you are successful and confident.

Remember, looking good isn't just about how others perceive you. It's about strategic presence, as we talked about in No. 73. Since people will often judge you based on their first thirty seconds of an encounter, there is no room for error.

BE STRATEGIC ABOUT YOUR BRAND AND REPUTATION; DON'T JUST LET IT HAPPEN.

Define what you want people to see, and then make sure that's who you are and what they see. Be strategic about your brand and reputation; don't just let it happen.

75.
CONSTANTLY PLANT SEEDS FOR YOUR FUTURE SUCCESS

Seeds grow. No seeds, no garden. Imagine what you want your future to be, then grow it into what you envision.

IMAGINE WHAT YOU WANT YOUR FUTURE TO BE, THEN GROW IT INTO WHAT YOU ENVISION.

Let me tell you a story I alluded to in the introduction. One of my mentors, Don Baker, told me twenty-one years ago when I moved into my estate where I live now (at the time of this writing) that I should plant small bushes and trees everywhere, even if I could only afford to pay $5 or $10 apiece for them. He said, "They will grow, and one day you'll have a forest that provides privacy and beautiful greenery around your estate." And that's exactly what we enjoy today.

The concept he taught me of planting seeds to be ready for the future has stayed with me, and I've taken it to another level of thinking. The seeds we plant could be for growing a person (like our kids, a member of our team, or a client) or growing our processes. Maybe you're working on constantly improving your processes now, and you'll be able to look back in two or three months and see that they're so much better. That's what I call planting seeds for the future!

76.
INVEST IN YOURSELF

Wouldn't you agree that Benjamin Franklin and Warren Buffett have known a few things about success? Their quotes listed at the beginning of this section say it all. Benjamin Franklin: "An investment in knowledge pays the best interest." Warren Buffett: "The best investment you can make is in yourself."

WISE PEOPLE WIN. READ GOOD BOOKS, ATTEND SEMINARS, STUDY POWERFUL VIDEOS, AND LEARN ALL YOU CAN.

Wise people win. Read good books, attend seminars, study powerful videos, and learn all you can. Prepare every day for your future. How much you prepare today determines who you will become in the future.

Most people don't invest in themselves like they should. When I'm giving a presentation, I often ask this question, "How much money and

HOW MUCH MONEY AND HOW MANY HOURS IN AN AVERAGE WEEK DID YOU INVEST IN YOURSELF IN THE LAST YEAR?

how many hours in an average week did you invest in yourself in the last year?" Most people answer, "Not enough." How about you? How much time and money do you invest in yourself?

77.
DIG FOR OPPORTUNITIES

This principle from Peter Thomas was included in the book we co-authored, *Business Ground Rules.* As we mentioned in the introduction, Peter is a super successful serial entrepreneur who has developed billions of dollars in real estate projects all across America and Canada. Here's how Peter explains his success:

Everyone who knows me knows my philosophy: There's a pony in there somewhere! This comes from an old story about a little boy who wanted a pony for Christmas. On Christmas morning, he woke up to find his Christmas tree surrounded not by gifts, but by a gigantic pile of manure. While all his friends stood around feeling sorry for him, knowing he didn't get what he wanted most, the little boy began wildly and happily digging through the pile of manure. "I just know there's a pony in there somewhere," he exclaimed.

> THERE ARE PONIES EVERYWHERE IF YOU ARE WILLING TO SHOVEL THE MANURE ASIDE. SOMETIMES IT SEEMS LIKE A LOT OF MANURE, BUT JUST KEEP SHOVELING WITH THE FAITH THAT THERE IS A PONY IN THERE SOMEWHERE.

That's how I've been all my life. My colleague, Charlie, watched me sort through and reject over 500 deals last summer when I started my newest venture, Thomas Franchise Solutions; and indeed, there was one pony in there: Dogtopia. It became our first deal.

In the early seventies, I "found" Century 21 Canada among all the possible deals I could have done.

In the eighties, I "found" literally hundreds of real estate projects and created Samoth Capital Corp. I put in all the properties I had created and took that organization public and raised hundreds of millions.

In the nineties, I "found" Westover Hills, one of the largest tracts of land in San Antonio, Texas, paying $9,000,000 and returning the partners over $120,000,000.

In 2000, I "found" the land to create The Four Seasons Hotel, in Phoenix, Arizona.

In 2012, I "found" Dogtopia and created Thomas Franchise Solutions.

I was not born wealthy; these opportunities just kept presenting themselves after a lot of digging. As the projects came, along came the wisdom to figure out how to do them, how to find the money, and how to find the partners.

My attitude says there are ponies everywhere if you are willing to shovel the manure aside. Sometimes it seems like a lot of manure, but just keep shoveling with the faith that there is a pony in there somewhere.

I am motivated by the thrill of the search. I want to succeed, and I want to find the perfect project. But it has to be the right project. I don't want to come up with a duck when I'm looking for that pony.

So when people call me or any of my successful entrepreneurial pals lucky, it's a special kind of luck: the luck of a person willing to work hard enough to get to the bottom of the pile and see what might be there, all the while believing in that pony.

Start digging!

> I WANT TO SUCCEED, AND I WANT TO FIND THE PERFECT PROJECT. BUT IT HAS TO BE THE RIGHT PROJECT.

78.
REWARD YOURSELF OFTEN

A pat on your own back goes a long way toward helping you prepare for your future.

Rewarding yourself is a great way to feel satisfaction about the things you're achieving and inspire yourself to do more. Pay yourself first. Buy a nice car, enjoy your hard work, take well-planned vacations.

> REWARDING YOURSELF IS A GREAT WAY TO FEEL SATISFACTION ABOUT THE THINGS YOU'RE ACHIEVING AND INSPIRE YOURSELF TO DO MORE.

Rewards can also be small things like sharing a concert with a friend, having a special date night, or purchasing a new gadget—anything that feels like a treat or reward to you. By doing those things, you'll be much less likely to burn out, because you will see the value in what you're working to achieve and what you're building.

We've all seen it: Some people go years without a vacation, only to find themselves burned out, stressed out, and unable to move forward. These are often the people who get so stuck that they want to quit what they're doing. They've worked so hard without a reward, only to find that they've lost their passion.

> KEEP THE REWARD IN FOCUS, BECAUSE IT WILL INSPIRE YOU TO WORK HARDER AND KEEP ON GOING.

Let's face it; we all enjoy knowing there's a reward coming soon. I encourage you to use a vision board, like I suggested in No. 15, to keep the reward in focus, because it will inspire you to work harder and keep on going. Ask yourself, *Do I keep rewards strategically in front of me to continually motivate and inspire me to reach my goals?* If not, you can start today.

79.
MANAGE YOUR ENERGY, NOT JUST YOUR TIME

One of my earliest books was one called *How to Gain 100 Extra Minutes a Day,* which was a great time-management book that I taught from for years. However, I realized several years ago that I was making a big mistake by not understanding that it's just as important to manage your energy as it is to manage your time. When you manage your energy, you have so much more capacity.

A huge piece to the puzzle is managing your high-energy times. So many people miss this one. If you want to be at your peak performance and get things done right, you must manage your high-energy times. One way to do that is to know whether you are a morning person, or whether your peak energy time is mid-day or evening. Then schedule your impactful opportunities on your calendar according to your high-energy times. Also understand that you can put yourself into high-energy states by playing music, by how you eat, by the people you're around, and by your environment. Create an environment and schedule for yourself so important minutes are managed to your advantage.

> IF YOU WANT TO BE AT YOUR PEAK PERFORMANCE AND GET THINGS DONE RIGHT, YOU MUST MANAGE YOUR HIGH-ENERGY TIMES.

X. HEALTH

*The foundation of success in life is good health: that is the
substratum fortune; it is also the basis of happiness.
A person cannot accumulate a fortune very well when he is sick.*
—P. T. BARNUM

The greatest wealth is health.
—VIRGIL

What is called genius is the abundance of life and health.
—HENRY DAVID THOREAU

80.
Prepare to Live Healthy

All results can be enhanced by being strategic, and that includes your health.

If you're unhealthy, both your personal and business lives can suffer, since you're not as strong as you need to be mentally or physically to multitask and operate with excellence. Few people take a strategic approach to their health by educating themselves on key areas that will result in a longer, higher quality life. If you're not as healthy as you should be, you need to ask yourself if you should be changing something.

> IF YOU'RE NOT AS HEALTHY AS YOU SHOULD BE, YOU NEED TO ASK YOURSELF IF YOU SHOULD BE CHANGING SOMETHING.

I authored a little book last year called *Strategic Health*, which was basically a summary of a book called *Ultimate Health* that I coauthored in 2013 with Dr. Rick Wilson, Dr. Jennifer Engels, and Tammy Kling. One of the catalysts for that book was the transformation I experienced when I started eliminating sugar and other unhealthy foods, monitoring calories, and focusing on a fitness regimen.

These books were based heavily on the journey I went through when I woke up one day and discovered, like so many, that I was out of shape, overweight, and not applying the concept of *Strategic Health* in my own life. I discovered how important knowledge—in particular, uncovering *Blind Spots*—is in mastering your health. I realized that I needed to change my thinking first, which had been largely influenced by commonly held yet outdated and erroneous ideas about health and fitness. In order to get clear on who I wanted to become, I went on a life *diet*, so to speak. I started consuming exceptional books on health and surrounding myself with the brightest minds in the medical and wellness fields to help me understand how the body really works and develop the habits I would need to build my health goals and actions around my vision.

I began educating myself on hormones, metabolism, exercise, diet, stress, and sleep, and I started seeing the huge impact it had on vitality, aging well, and my overall health results. I reduced my weight by forty pounds (20 percent of my whole body, gone), my body fat from 25 percent to 10 percent, and my telomere age (cellular age) from that of a fifty-year-old to one of a twenty-seven-year-old.

Strategic Health is getting clear on who you want to become and then building your health goals and actions around that vision. Health is a super structure upon which success and quality of life rest. Read on to get some of our best strategies for achieving success in some of the foundational pillars that support that super structure.

STRATEGIC HEALTH IS GETTING CLEAR ON WHO YOU WANT TO BECOME AND THEN BUILDING YOUR HEALTH GOALS AND ACTIONS AROUND THAT VISION.

81.
PREVENT DISEASE BY CONTROLLING YOUR DIET

Everyone eats. Some eat smartly. Few eat strategically.

How old do you want to be when you die? And, more important-ly, how healthy, active, and fulfilled do you want to be until that time comes?

A substantial part of healthy living is your diet, which has a significant impact on how old you will be when you die and the quality of life you will lead until that day.

A SUBSTANTIAL PART OF HEALTHY LIVING IS YOUR DIET, WHICH HAS A SIGNIFICANT IMPACT ON HOW OLD YOU WILL BE WHEN YOU DIE AND THE QUALITY OF LIFE YOU WILL LEAD UNTIL THAT DAY.

Look around you. How many adults are in great shape and mentally happy? Very few people retain those youthful qualities into adulthood. To do so re-quires a shift in thinking—filling your mind with positive, empowering infor-mation centered on living a healthy life-style.

What you know and how you approach your diet can elevate your health to the next level. By following these simple strategies, you will form a great new picture of your life and your future. First, you should know what you need and decide where the level is, and from that you need to figure out how you can leverage your thinking to help you max-imize each strategy.

Calories: Know how many calories your body requires on a normal daily basis. Knowledge allows you to make better daily choices. Some foods will leave you feeling hungry and tired shortly after eating them, and others provide fuel that will get your mind and body operating more efficiently. If weight loss is your goal, simply burn off more calo-ries than you put in.

Carbs: Choose carbs that have a low glycemic index and are high in fiber. When in doubt, do a quick online search and see where your desired food lands on the GI Scale. If it's higher than 55, take a minute to consider whether you need that food in your diet or you can replace it with a smarter food option. If you still want it, reduce your portion by half.

Timing: Timing is everything. When you eat can be just as important as what you eat. Front-load your day and slow down at night. Dinner should be your lightest meal and should be consumed no less than three hours before bedtime. Eating too late at night forces your body to work unnaturally, because your metabolism slows down when you sleep, which pushes your body to work harder to break foods down.

Sugar: The regular consumption of sugary foods is one of the worst things you can do for Strategic Health. Modern scientific research has shown that sugar—in all its myriad forms—is taking a devastating toll on our health. Excess intake of all processed sugars results in compromised immune function, obesity, and diabetes.

Water: Water consumption is imperative for maintaining hydration and being strategic about your health. Generally speaking, women should drink 11 cups (90 ounces) of water per day and men should drink 16 cups (125 ounces) per day.

REMEMBER, YOU TRULY ARE WHAT YOU EAT. ASK YOURSELF IF THE WAY YOU'RE EATING NOW WILL PREPARE YOU FOR THE FUTURE YOU WANT.

You should not be *dieting*; rather, your *diet* should be a lifestyle. Technically, "diet" simply refers to the foods you eat on a regular basis. So when people say they are "dieting," they mean they are *temporarily* eating healthier to lose weight. Instead of "dieting" for the short term, you can create realistic, achievable goals that are sustainable for the long term.

Remember, you truly are what you eat. Ask yourself if the way you're eating now will prepare you for the future you want.

82.
PREPARE FOR QUALITY OF LIFE WITH THE RIGHT EXERCISE

Getting active with regular, daily exercise is one of the best ways to boost your immune system. There are many studies that validate the truth that the risk for all causes of mortality and serious disease, including heart disease, cancer, and diabetes, is lowered by being physically fit. The science is there. Exercise heals.

Aerobics: Aerobic fitness and cardiovascular conditioning has been proven by medical researchers to play a major role in both quality of life and prolongation of life. Cardiovascular exercise increases cells that fight infection, so even a brisk walk or jog is beneficial. When you increase your heart rate, you get an infusion of endorphins to fight stress, and a flood of mood-enhancing chemicals along with them.

> THE RISK FOR ALL CAUSES OF MORTALITY AND SERIOUS DISEASE, INCLUDING HEART DISEASE, CANCER, AND DIABETES, IS LOWERED BY BEING PHYSICALLY FIT. THE SCIENCE IS THERE. EXERCISE HEALS.

Resistance training: As we get older, we tend to lose muscle and gain fat—and our metabolism slows down as a result. One way to combat this metabolic slowdown is with regular strength or resistance training. Resistance training stimulates muscles to become stronger and healthier, providing your body with beneficial improvements in strength and function.

Stretching: Stretching is an often overlooked, yet essential component of a great workout routine. Stretching keeps the muscles flexible, strong, and healthy, and we need that flexibility to maintain a range of motion in the joints. Not stretching causes your muscles to become short and tight, which puts you at risk for joint pain, strains, and muscle damage.

Balance: Balance exercises have been proven to help older adults improve overall mobility, function, and mental health, while reducing symptoms and discomfort of chronic conditions such as arthritis. The core is the balance center in the body. Maintaining a strong core allows you to control your body's posture, positioning, and stability, and helps you maintain an upright position.

PHYSICAL EXERCISE—REGULAR, FREQUENT, AND ONGOING—MATTERS.

Physical exercise—regular, frequent, and ongoing—matters. Strength resistance, cardiovascular exercise (aerobics), balance, and stretching all promote a better-operating body. Are you strategically building the best operating body you need to get the life results you want?

83.
MANAGE STRESS BY BEING CLEAR AHEAD ON WHAT MATTERS AND WHERE YOU ARE

One of the major causes of disease, aging, and death is stress. Stress occurs when your mental, physical, or spiritual challenges exceed your ability to cope with them. Stress kills—literally. It causes your body to secrete hormones (cortisol and adrenaline) that can have a negative impact on your health.

Your adrenal glands produce several hormones, one of which is cortisol, a stress-related hormone. A little is good for normal functioning; however, if your adrenal glands secrete the hormone too much and too often, the surplus has damaging health effects, such as increased tissue inflammation, elevated blood pressure, and decreased immunity.

Are you managing anxiety and making a conscious effort to eliminate stress? Is your life aligned with your values? Have you set up harmony in your home, office, and life so things run as smoothly as possible? Is your pace of life contributing to or detracting from your overall well-being?

Stress is often caused because of lack of clarity about your future. When you are clear on what really matters and where you are going, you can make the best decisions about what to avoid and when and how to take action and move ahead.

People often don't realize why something works when you write it down. Writing down your goals is a powerful concept. When you write something down there's a pulling power that happens, and you're really preparing yourself to receive it, enjoy it, and make it a part of who you are.

> WRITING DOWN YOUR GOALS IS A POWERFUL CONCEPT. THERE'S A PULLING POWER THAT HAPPENS, AND YOU'RE REALLY PREPARING YOURSELF TO RECEIVE IT, ENJOY IT, AND MAKE IT A PART OF WHO YOU ARE.

84.
A HEALTHY LIFE INCLUDES WHAT YOU THINK ABOUT, LET GO OF, AND REFUSE TO BELIEVE

Strategic Health is about achieving success in multiple areas of your life—mentally, physically, emotionally, spiritually, and even financially. Living a healthy life is about more than just what you eat and how often you exercise. It is also about what you think, let go of, and refuse to believe (for example, things others have said to or about you that have lowered your self-worth or your belief capacity). Your mind and body are intertwined, and what goes into one affects the other.

> LIVING A HEALTHY LIFE IS ABOUT MORE THAN JUST WHAT YOU EAT AND HOW OFTEN YOU EXERCISE. IT IS ALSO ABOUT WHAT YOU THINK, LET GO OF, AND REFUSE TO BELIEVE.

Strategic Health for your mind includes being conscious about eliminating toxins, such as unproductive thought patterns, unhealthy habits, and negative and self-limiting beliefs, and increasing positive thoughts, energy, and momentum. It encompasses being intentional about who you spend time with, because the people around you greatly impact your success. *Strategic Health* is an active process of developing essential daily habits that are restorative and transformative—habits that lead to a vibrant, energetic life for decades to come.

85.
Remove Toxins to Stay Healthy

If you want to prepare for success in every area of your life, you must become aware of and eliminate toxins—and that can be stress, chemicals, people, habits, attitudes, or anything else that drags you down and keeps you from being the best you can be.

Chemical toxins, especially, are pervasive in our environment and in our bodies and can be linked to just about every chronic and autoimmune disease. So how do we stay healthy despite the prevalence of these substances? Our bodies are designed to filter out toxins, and yet we can put ourselves at an advantage if we avoid chemical toxins altogether.

Here are a few suggestions for removing toxins—chemical and otherwise:

> CHEMICAL TOXINS, ESPECIALLY, ARE PERVASIVE IN OUR ENVIRONMENT AND IN OUR BODIES AND CAN BE LINKED TO JUST ABOUT EVERY CHRONIC AND AUTOIMMUNE DISEASE.

- Eat organic
- Use green cleaning products
- Freshen your air with essential oils, house plants, and a high-quality air filter
- Use nontoxic, naturally based beauty products
- Install a quality water filter
- Reduce microwave use
- Ditch the Teflon
- Cook with healthier oils, like coconut oil and ghee
- Sweat it out with an infrared sauna, traditional cedar sauna, or hot yoga
- Choose to spend your time with inspirational and energizing people

• Manage your cash flow well

How many toxins do you need to eliminate from your life to prepare yourself for your best future?

86.
MAKE THE BEST USE OF SUPPLEMENTS

Your body functions at an ideal state when nutrition and lifestyle are aligned to put it in balance with key areas such as hormones, nourishment levels, PH levels, etc. Generally speaking, most people don't eat at a level of discipline to put their body at an ideal state in all of these areas. Therefore, adopting a daily supplementation system is a smart choice. The more you understand your body chemistry and the more you educate yourself on the different qualities of products in the marketplace, the better choices you can make to achieve optimal health.

> ADOPTING A DAILY SUPPLEMENTATION SYSTEM IS A SMART CHOICE TO HELP YOU PUT YOUR BODY AT AN IDEAL STATE.

Here are a few suggestions that may help you:

• Test your hormonal status and supplement where you need to.

• Supplement with vitamins and minerals when your diet lacks nutritional balance, especially with whole, raw food sources and ample vegetable servings. Your physician can tell you what you need to take on a daily basis after testing your blood.

• Use probiotics to help to support your immune system, fight against "bad bacteria," and help your body digest and absorb nutrients.

• Supplement with fish oils to lower blood pressure and triglycerides, help prevent asthma, relieve joint pain and stiffness, help quell gastrointestinal inflammation, and possibly prevent Alzheimer's disease. Essential fatty acids (omega-3 and omega-6s) are essential to Strategic Health.

Put simply, supplements enhance your health. If you want to be your best, work with your physician, endocrinologist, or other qualified practitioner to determine what supplements are best for you.

X. ARSENAL

A good coach will have an arsenal of tools to share with you.
—TONY JEARY

*Technology is nothing. What's important is that you have a
faith in people, that they're basically good and smart,
and if you give them tools, they'll do wonderful things with them.*
—STEVE JOBS

The stronger your arsenal, the faster the results you'll get.
—TONY JEARY

87.
THE BIGGER YOUR ARSENAL THE MORE LEVERAGE YOU HAVE

Having the right tools at the right time can make a world of difference in preparing for your success. Keeping an arsenal of tools helps you present your messaging, it helps you and your team execute faster, and it makes you more valuable as a leader.

When you have tools, you're taking a proactive approach. You don't have to recreate the wheel each time you want to do something. However, it takes energy and effort to plan ahead, sort, and organize now for something you might not use for years. If you think about it, you're already building a mental arsenal of things like your connections, books and articles you've read, and movies you've seen—things that naturally occur. You just may need to be more strategic in the way you collect and file things on your computer.

> KEEPING AN ARSENAL OF TOOLS HELPS YOU PRESENT YOUR MESSAGING, IT HELPS YOU AND YOUR TEAM EXECUTE FASTER, AND IT MAKES YOU MORE VALUABLE AS A LEADER.

As a leader, you should have a big toolbox for your organization. If you don't know where to start, make a list of the things people want from you. Instead of recreating the wheel, develop a tool mindset. Do you need an app? Do you need a book? What tools do your competitors have that you don't?

Create an arsenal you can send to clients as well. In our office, we obviously create books, DVDs, book recaps, and even goal-setting or business-plan templates, among other things, that we give away to clients to help them win. We give people tools that will help them succeed at business, team building, development, or strategy. When they win, we win.

An arsenal can consist of a list of powerful URLs or videos, books,

AN ARSENAL CAN CONSIST OF A LIST OF POWERFUL URLS OR VIDEOS, BOOKS, SUMMARIES, PICTURES, BEST PRACTICES, QUOTES, TRUISMS, WHITEPAPERS, EXAMPLES, CASE STUDIES, ANIMATIONS, AND MORE. THE MORE ROBUST YOUR ARSENAL, THE BETTER EQUIPPED YOU WILL BE TO RESPOND TO EVERY SITUATION.

summaries, pictures, best practices, quotes, truisms, whitepapers, examples, case studies, animations, and more. Just like a military arsenal, the idea is to "arm" yourself to respond quickly. Start now, and then little by little, week by week, month by month, you can intentionally build a powerful arsenal. The more robust it is, the better equipped you will be to respond to every situation.

88.
FOCUS ON CREATING EXTRA VALUE BY BUILDING A STRONG ARSENAL / TOOL CHEST IN ADVANCE

It's easier to exceed expectations if you've planned ahead and have accumulated and organized valuable mental, physical, and electronic arsenals.

For example, if you have extra books in your physical arsenal, when you go to lunch with someone you could take a book that person likes. Suddenly you become more valuable in their eyes, your brand is stronger, and, in my opinion, you're a bigger component of that person's success. If you had not prepared ahead and had those books on hand, you probably wouldn't have burned the time to run by the bookstore and buy a book to take to someone you're meeting for lunch.

> IT'S EASIER TO EXCEED EXPECTATIONS IF YOU'VE PLANNED AHEAD AND HAVE ACCUMULATED AND ORGANIZED VALUABLE MENTAL, PHYSICAL, AND ELECTRONIC ARSENALS.

A big part of the best practice of having a physical arsenal, then, is to plan to have things on hand in advance. When I go to Asia, I often buy ten or twenty of some of the cool items I find and bring them back for my arsenal. Then, when kids come to my office or home, I can go to my box and hand them a gift. Over the years that has become a fun practice.

Of course, you can also put things in your electronic arsenal on your phone to share with others, which could include some of the things we mentioned in No. 87 (lists of powerful URLs, pictures, quotes, truisms, etc.).

Develop a mindset that's constantly asking, *How can I prepare ahead to enrich my arsenal so I can help other people win?*

89.
YOU HAVE LESS STRESS WITH A MORE SOLVABLE TOOL CHEST

My *Life Team* is a huge, valuable part of my arsenal, and it should be part of yours, too. (In No. 39 we talked about the value of building your *Life Team*—people who help you extend your ability to get things done, make better decisions, and do more of what you love.) You create wins for yourself and others when you keep a list of proven vendors and contractors and their phone numbers so they're immediately accessible in your electronic arsenal. Then when you or someone you know is stuck and don't know how to fix something, you can reach for your phone and pull up the number of the right person to get the task done.

> YOU CREATE WINS FOR YOURSELF AND OTHERS WHEN YOU KEEP A LIST OF PROVEN VENDORS AND CONTRACTORS AND THEIR PHONE NUMBERS SO THEY'RE IMMEDIATELY ACCESSIBLE IN YOUR ELECTRONIC ARSENAL.

A few weeks ago I needed to move something; and since I have my *Life Team* members in my electronic arsenal, I was able to make one phone call to make that happen. Because I had that solvable tool chest, it was, frankly, much less stressful.

I might note that I not only had the connections to get it done: I had also done *Favors in Advance* that allowed me to get it accomplished at no cost (see No. 41). Doing *Favors in Advance* creates community, where people are willing to help each other out. That's a powerful thing to have in your arsenal!

90.
BUILD A LIST OF FUN, VALUABLE PUBLIC DOMAIN URLS

If you don't want to burn tons of money on giving things away, you can still have a valuable, organized arsenal that doesn't cost much money by collecting great URLs. For example, if you want to be funnier or stronger in your staff meetings, just prepare ahead with a list of easy-to-get-to public-domain video links and URLs—a set of resources to support your being humorous and more valuable to your team. Some of the URLs could be websites and some could be powerful videos. Last weekend, a friend sent me a video of something I wanted to watch. It was valuable for me, and it took him just a few seconds to forward it to me.

IF YOU DON'T WANT TO BURN TONS OF MONEY ON GIVING THINGS AWAY, YOU CAN STILL HAVE A VALUABLE, ORGANIZED ARSENAL THAT DOESN'T COST MUCH MONEY BY COLLECTING GREAT URLS.

Here's another great example: I recently found a beautiful website on summaries of the Bible: https://overviewbible.com/books-of-the-bible. First, it gives in 144 words or less a description of each book of the Bible; then, if you want to go deeper, you can click on a button that takes you into more detail about each book. I was so pleased to find it within just a couple of clicks after I did a search for "summary of the books of the Bible." From an arsenal standpoint, if you wanted to minister to someone by giving them an understanding of the Bible, you could send them this URL. You would certainly be doing the person a favor by helping them get a grasp of the Bible without having the benefit of the years of study that many of us have put into it.

By having a list of great URLs ahead of time, you're always prepared to exceed the expectations of your clients, friends, and family.

91.
INCLUDE A PICTURE OF YOUR FAMILY'S GOALS WALL IN YOUR ARSENAL

One of the greatest personal tools I have in my arsenal is a picture of my family's goals wall (also called a vision board—see No. 15 for a picture). I keep a current picture on my phone, because it's a great motivator for my clients or someone I'm talking to about the power of visualization. (If you do a search for "Tony Jeary Results Boarding," you'll find a two-minute video about the impact of visualizing with a results board.)

My family's goals board not only serves as a motivator for other people. It's also a place where we assemble an arsenal of pictures of the places we want to go and things we want to do as a family; it inspires us to reach our goals of things we want to have, share, experience, give, and become.

XII. FORCE MULTIPLIERS

One of the most powerful scientific tools ever invented is the telephone.
—JOHN C. MATHER

*Force multipliers help you leverage to get things done faster
and more efficiently, and hence get better results.*
—TONY JEARY

92.
YOUR PHONE IS A HUGE FORCE MULTIPLIER

A force multiplier is a factor that dramatically increases (multiplies) the effectiveness of something you're doing. In the military, it's a term that applies to a capability that significantly increases the combat potential of a military force and thus enhances the probability of a successful mission. One example would be night goggles. If a combat force goes into a particular area at night, night goggles would significantly enhance their chances of a successful mission.

A force multiplier, then, is really about leverage. I believe that in today's world, your phone is one of the most effective force multipliers you can have. Utilized correctly, it can be leveraged to prepare you to get immensely better results, faster. I want to take you to a new place in the way you think about your phone—a place where few people go—so you can be prepared to multiply your results.

> IN TODAY'S WORLD, YOUR PHONE IS ONE OF THE MOST EFFECTIVE FORCE MULTIPLIERS YOU CAN HAVE. UTILIZED CORRECTLY, IT CAN BE LEVERAGED TO PREPARE YOU TO GET IMMENSELY BETTER RESULTS, FASTER.

Consider the impact on your results if you employ these usages of your phone:

1. Use the notes feature to keep lists on your phone. Making lists is a key to organization (see No. 100), and putting your lists on your phone is crucial to making your lists work for you. Be sure your phone is organized so you can get to them quickly. Make sure you include:
   - Your goals—not just what you want to have, but also what you want to share, experience, give, and of course become. Keeping them on your phone helps you visualize them often, which serves as a motivator.

- Your spouse's goals. If you happen to be married, write down the things that are important to your spouse. Refer to them often to see how you can support their goals.

- Your kids' goals. If you have kids, no matter their age, ask them what you can do to support their goals this year (it's a great opening to discuss their goals with them). Again, look at them often to remind you of your commitment to support them.

- Your HLAs. Remember, nothing has a more powerful impact on results than focusing on your High Leverage Activities (see No. 13), so make sure you write down your HLAs in your phone, both personal and professional, and look at them several times a day.

- Your to-do list. You want to be able to look at your to-do list throughout the day, as well, and ask yourself, *What's the best use of my time right now?*

- Your daily performance standards (see No. 12).

- *Life Team* (see No. 39). Make sure you have a very organized list of your *Life Team* members on your phone as well as on your computer, indicating their role along with their name and contact information. Having that information on your phone saves a ton of time when you need something done right away.

- *People of Influence.* List your POIs (see No. 49), along with their goals and ambitions and how they want you to support them. I teach my high achievers to do this, because it is such a huge piece of getting results faster. Putting your list of POIs on your phone will trigger reminders to connect with them on a regular basis.

- A travel checklist (see No. 95) that will help you remember to pack all the things you need.

2. Use the software and apps on your phone as part of your electronic tool chest.

3. Keep your contacts on your phone. I have my staff electronically feed our contacts' name and information into a software program

so my team and I can have them on our phones as well as in our computers. You should, too, so you can effectively keep up with and nourish all the different connections and relationships you have.

4. Do a SWOT (an assessment of your strengths, weaknesses, opportunities, and threats) on yourself and write down your answers in your phone. Then you can look at it several times a year and ask yourself, *Am I really exploiting my strengths? Am I uncovering and sharpening my weaknesses? Am I really taking my opportunities to the highest level and getting better? And am I making sure I cover for any threats?*

> YOUR PHONE COULD EASILY BE TODAY'S SINGLE BIGGEST FORCE MULTIPLIER IN THE ELECTRIC TOOL CATEGORY.

5. Keep your MOLO assessment (see No. 11) on your phone as a constant reminder of what you want more of and what you want less of.

6. Daily huddles with your team. Do you have a consistent habit of daily calibrating your team—by phone or in person—so you can have synchronized focus and clarity of priorities?

Your phone could easily be today's single biggest force multiplier in the electric tool category. Be sure to keep it in good working order so you can be prepared and ready at all times.

93.
USE DROPBOX OR AN ONLINE SYSTEM

There's nothing that sabotages preparation more than losing files. Using Dropbox or an online system to back up your files—one that is consistently updated and ready to be an extension of you, your business, and your life—is not optional if you want to be prepared for anything that could happen. It not only saves you time that would otherwise be wasted on looking for lost items; it could also save an important business opportunity!

There are many services to choose from. Just make sure you use a system that you can access from any of your devices so you can share files with others any time from anywhere. Your clients will love it! Preparation pays!

> USING DROPBOX OR AN ONLINE SYSTEM TO BACK UP YOUR FILES—ONE THAT IS CONSISTENTLY UPDATED AND READY TO BE AN EXTENSION OF YOU, YOUR BUSINESS, AND YOUR LIFE—IS NOT OPTIONAL IF YOU WANT TO BE PREPARED FOR ANYTHING THAT COULD HAPPEN.

94.
TAKE STRATEGIC NOTES

A GOOD NOTES TEMPLATE IS AN EXCELLENT TOOL THAT CAN LITERALLY CHANGE THE DYNAMICS OF YOUR PREPARATION.

Prepare for helping both yourself and others in the future by being strategic in the way you take notes. You might initially handwrite the VIP's (very important points) of the meeting, phone call, speaking event, etc., and then type them up later so you can save them for yourself and/or email them to others, so you're bringing value into their lives.

Strategic notetaking is also vital for the purpose of retention. Hermann Ebbinghaus, the first psychologist to study learning and memory, taught that you can move things into your long-term memory by reviewing them one day, then seven days, and then six months after you originally learned them.

In our office, we're very strategic about taking good notes in meetings. We've developed an excellent notes template that we fill in throughout the meeting; then we send it to all the participants later so they can see all of the pertinent pieces. Much of it can be prepared in advance. At the top of our notes template, we list who is in attendance; then we list the objectives, the agenda, the expectations, and the most important points. Then we fill in who is supposed to take action, along with the actions they're going to take and by what date. And finally we list any closing comments. A good notes template is an excellent tool that can literally change the dynamics of your preparation.

BUILD AND USE CHECKLISTS

The mind is a powerful thing, and yet it's not always perfect. We often forget things and let things fall through the cracks. That's why checklists are so powerful. Any time you want to prepare for a trip, a meeting, or for virtually any kind of experience, consider adopting proven checklists (like a preflight checklist for a pilot), or building your own.

Use checklists on a consistent, ongoing basis to support always being organized and prepared.

XIII. HABITS

If you're going to achieve excellence in big things,
you develop the habit in little matters.
Excellence is not an exception; it is a prevailing attitude.
—COLIN POWELL

Motivation is what gets you started.
Habit is what keeps you going.
—JIM RYUN

Winning is habit. Unfortunately, so is losing.
—VINCE LOMBARDI

True realism consists in revealing the surprising things
which habit keeps covered and prevents us from seeing.
—JEAN COCTEAU

96.
Notice Patterns and Turn Them into the Right Habits

As you're preparing to go to the next level of success, it's critical to remember that habits matter. In fact, the results we get in our lives can be directly attributed to the habits we form.

Habits, both good and bad, need to be strategically managed for anyone desiring to operate in the highest level. Habits are powerful, and they're a huge part of the success puzzle. Developing good habits allows you to master the things in life that are important to you and helps you weed out bad habits. The bottom line is, good habits make you more productive and set you up to better succeed.

THE RESULTS WE GET IN OUR LIVES CAN BE DIRECTLY ATTRIBUTED TO THE HABITS WE FORM.

Carefully notice, identify, and reflect on the patterns in your life. Actually, your brain has a mechanism that helps you do that unconsciously to a certain extent. At the center of your brain is a walnut-sized piece of "neural tissue" called the basal ganglia, which basically offloads from the cerebral cortex (the "thinking" part of the brain) any sequences that have turned into systems/habits, therefore freeing the cerebral

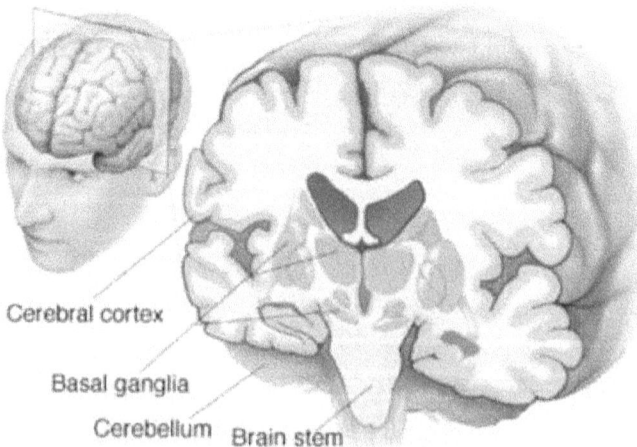

Cerebral cortex

Basal ganglia

Cerebellum Brain stem

cortex up to handle other things. So the brain actually craves habits and systems so it doesn't have to work so hard!

You can help the basal ganglia along by consciously identifying your patterns, and then either reinforcing or changing them as needed, based on the results you're getting versus the results you desire. If you like the results of something you're doing, keep doing it; if you don't like the results, do something different. Remember, frequency, less friction, and simplicity lead to habit achievement.

Here's another angle: By doing a "life audit" and making a list of the top ten most stressful things that happen on a daily basis, you can often discover a lot of habits and processes—or lack thereof—that could be modified. By changing certain habits, you can eliminate most sources of stress in your life. Your true wealth is determined by the number of things you don't have to worry about. Worry is a stressor.

Bad habits don't produce winners. Great habits prepare you for and guide you to success.

> BY DOING A "LIFE AUDIT" AND MAKING A LIST OF THE TOP TEN MOST STRESSFUL THINGS THAT HAPPEN ON A DAILY BASIS, YOU CAN OFTEN DISCOVER A LOT OF HABITS AND PROCESSES—OR LACK THEREOF—THAT COULD BE MODIFIED.

97.
Think Like Successful People Think and Do What Successful People Do

I'm not advocating for success as it applies only to material wealth, although it's good to have money, because money can offer you freedom. Money is a blessing and you often need it to fuel your dreams. So if financial freedom and growing monetary wealth are your goals, that's great. I prefer to live wealthy (successful) in all areas of life. I call it *Living in the Black* (which is the name of a book I authored several years ago).

In order to prepare yourself to get money and create wealth (however you define it), you need to think how successful people think. If you keep running into brick walls and you're not sure why, find someone who is truly wealthy and emulate their philosophies. You could tap a business owner you've admired from afar, or it might be a family friend or an elder. I suggest you interview that individual about their thought patterns, life and business outlooks, and personal style. Then model that person and live the way they live.

WEALTHY, SUCCESSFUL PEOPLE HAVE SPECIFIC, DAILY HABITS IN COMMON, AND SO DO POOR PEOPLE WHO ARE UNSUCCESSFUL.

I've found that there are often extreme differences, particularly in habits, between people who are successful and those who are not. Wealthy, successful people have specific, daily habits in common, and so do poor people who are unsuccessful.

I believe that most successful people:

- Have a routine: They rise early, start the day with purpose, nourish themselves regularly, and have other predictable behaviors.

- Are disciplined: They meet deadlines, deliver on promises, and keep their word.

- Concentrate on overall well-being: They care for their bodies, minds, and businesses, and they treat them like the irreplaceable tools they are.

- Have focus: They figure out what needs to be done and stay on track through the activities that matter most.

- Continually learn: They read, engage mentors, or advance their education; then they find ways to incorporate what they've learned into their lives.

- Stay positive: They look on the bright side, are solution-oriented, and seek success instead of dwelling on misery.

What are some habits you can refine or adopt that mirror those of successful, wealthy people you admire most?

98.
PREPARE TO LIVE AT THE HIGHEST LEVEL BY EXECUTING TO THE POINT OF HABIT

For decades I've worked with and advised the highest achievers across industries all over the world; and I've come to believe that there are three basic steps for preparing to live at the highest level in your business, parenting, marriage, leadership, mentoring, health, or any other facet of your life:

Step one: You have to be aware of the different levels (good, great and mastery) and know at what level you're currently operating.

Step two: You must understand the benefits of living at the mastery level so your "want-to factor" kicks into high gear. Then you are self-inspired and motivated because you truly understand the feelings you can experience by living at this success level.

> ANY OF US CAN ACHIEVE MASTERY IN ANY AREA OF OUR LIVES IF WE'RE TRULY WILLING TO COMMIT OUR HABITS TO IT ENTIRELY.

Step three: You must execute to the point of habit, where the right things (in both thinking and doing) become automatic (see No. 99). Your habits allow you to produce incredible results over and over.

Any of us can achieve mastery in any area of our lives if we're truly willing to commit our habits to it entirely. And that includes habitually raising our (clearly documented) standards and not tolerating anything less than the very best. This is what it takes to be a true master.

99.
BE STRATEGIC ABOUT MOVING THINGS INTO THE AUTOMATIC ZONE

I believe the best preparation for success in life comes with the freedom to have built-in margin time so you can put your efforts and energies where you want them. If you want to live at the highest level, then you have to be strategic and intentional about moving things into the automatic zone; and that, of course, involves habits.

You can get more automatic by setting systems in place for things other people do for you and by allowing technology to take over some of the tactical things in your life—even using something as simple as a sprinkler system. One day I realized that my sprinkler system could be expanded to automate another task besides keeping my lawn, trees, and shrubs watered. I added a zone to fill my pool, so the pool now gets filled automatically every day. Making tasks happen automatically frees you up for other, more important things. When I get a long-term prescription, I have it mailed to me monthly, and I do the same with my supplements. I put everything I can on automatic. I'm blessed with a home team that handles my clothes. I even have an automatic system for dry cleaning; when I set my clothes out, they go out to the cleaners. When they come back, I have people who put them in my closet and keep it organized. I automate everything I can with habits, and I want you to think about that as well.

The real impact comes when you automate not only the tasks that others and technology can do for you, but also the foundational things you do for yourself that can accelerate your success. Habits are a way of putting yourself on autopilot or automatic, yet they are so much more. They can be pre-directed so the end result is what you really want.

Remember, the results we get in life can be directly attributed to the habits we form. We continue in our habits because we crave and reward the outcomes. Think about it. How often do you keep a bad habit because you crave what it gives you? Here's a profound truth: You have to strategically lift up and see the big picture, and then make whatever changes are necessary to improve your habits. If you're intentional about developing good habits, you will eventually replace the bad habits. It's like growing grass. If you grow grass, it chokes out the weeds. If you put good habits in, you can choke out your bad habits. Getting rid of bad habits by bringing in more good habits is a big piece of the preparation puzzle.

WE CONTINUE IN OUR HABITS BECAUSE WE CRAVE AND REWARD THE OUTCOMES. YOU HAVE TO STRATEGICALLY LIFT UP AND SEE THE BIG PICTURE, AND THEN MAKE WHATEVER CHANGES ARE NECESSARY TO IMPROVE YOUR HABITS.

100.
CREATE FOUNDATIONAL HABITS

In my own life, I deploy six strategic foundational habits. And I teach these same powerful habits to my high achieving clients, because I know they can help them live in that mastery level. I want to share these strategic six with you right now:

1. **Strategic list making and list managing.** I'm not talking about just daily to-dos; I'm talking about putting every single thing you do into a list format—your HLAs, your goals, your spouse's goals, your kids' goals, your POIs, your Life Team, etc. So many people think, I can remember this, so they don't write it down. That just fills up and chokes your mind. You can release things from your mind when you put them down in a list, because you know you can go back and look at them later.

> YOU CAN RELEASE THINGS FROM YOUR MIND WHEN YOU PUT THEM DOWN IN A LIST, BECAUSE YOU KNOW YOU CAN GO BACK AND LOOK AT THEM LATER.

If you form the habit of looking at your to-do list ten or twelve times a day, then you don't get to the end of the day and think, How did I do? Throughout the day you see that you're accomplishing the things you should. In fact, it's a good idea to strategically look at your list sometime during mid-afternoon each day and ask, How many of my priorities have I accomplished, and what do I have left? Then you can take the last few hours of your day and really get going to make sure you end the day with the most important things completed.

2. **Strategic goal setting.** I am passionate about goal setting, and I teach and preach to my clients that you have to be strategic about it. In fact, if you want to succeed at the highest level, it's crucial that you make goal setting one of your strategic habits—something you do habitually every week or every quarter or every year. If you establish it as a strategic habit, then you'll do it whether you feel inspired to or not. When you have an effective goal-setting system, you can look at it every few

days and see how you're progressing and then adjust it accordingly.

3. **Strategic health.** We can have everything in the world, and yet if we don't have our health, does it really matter? There are two specific elements involved here:

a. Exercise habits

b. The right eating habits

If you don't exercise, you won't have a healthy body. If you don't eat right, you won't have a healthy body. You need to examine every bite you put in your body, even down to the point of being strategic about your snacking. Set up the habits that will help you be the healthiest.

> IF YOU WANT TO SUCCEED AT THE HIGHEST LEVEL, IT'S CRUCIAL THAT YOU MAKE GOAL SETTING ONE OF YOUR STRATEGIC HABITS—SOMETHING YOU DO HABITUALLY EVERY WEEK OR EVERY QUARTER OR EVERY YEAR.

4. **Strategic learning.** Are you habitual about putting things into your life that will help you learn? For example, when you subscribe to magazines or blogs that support your goals, you're putting things on automatic mode that will help you habitually learn. Almost every night, I read and watch videos that will help me learn. I often go to bed watching bios, because I like to hear about other people's success stories and learn their distinctions. And lately I've taken my strategic learning up a notch. When I hear distinctions that apply to me as I'm listening to those bios, I list those distinctions in my phone.

I'm so into strategically managing my habits that I've figured out how to combine two of them into an *Elegant Solution.* I've put a flipchart in my gym, and I've asked my trainers, while they're setting up for me in the mornings, to write out things on the flipchart I can be learning. Then between sets I go over and learn. Strategic learning, strategic health.

5. **Strategic altruism.** That's being automatic about constantly encouraging, supporting, helping, and doing things for others. As you go

through life, do you have a habit of helping other people?

6. **Strategic willpower.** Willpower is like a muscle. It can grow big, and it can get tired. With the right management it can be strengthened to positively impact your decisions, like the decision to eat correctly. Develop the habit of eating every two hours so you don't let yourself get super hungry, because if you do you gorge and then overeat until you feel stuffed. We've all been there, and we all know what it's like not to have that discipline. Establishing the habit of willpower and managing it is an important piece.

How are you doing on these six strategic habits? Did you find there's room for improvement? All six are crucial as you prepare for a higher level of success.

CONCLUSION

As you read through this book, I hope you could see that preparation pays huge dividends! And in all the thirteen categories and 100 topics, I trust you were able to pinpoint at least a few areas in which you could improve your level of preparation to help you get the results you want, faster.

Look back at the chart in the introduction in which you rated your level of preparation in each of the categories. Now that you've read through the book, some things may have popped out that you realize you could do better on, or you may have realized you're already doing better than you originally thought. I've repeated the chart below so you can look at it again and see if you need to change any of your ratings—either higher or lower.

	Category	Description	Rating
1.	Clarity	Start with clarity about your vision, goals, values, purpose, and standards; create a written plan and MOLO your life often.	
2.	Focus	Sharpen and maintain your focus; eliminate distractions; focus on results vs. activities.	
3.	Execution	Be intentional: Dwell on solutions, communicate your vision, measure everything, execute with speed, and use powerful self-talk.	
4.	Time Mindset	Manage your time by saying "no" often, creating *Elegant Solutions*, and prioritizing hourly; have a "do-it-now" attitude.	
5.	Thinking	Value daily thinking time; get a great coach and mentors to help you discover your *Blind Spots*; and understand you become what you think about.	
6.	Relationships	Rich relationships = rich life. Surround yourself with a powerful *Life Team* and positive, successful people; nourish your relationships; do *Favors in Advance*.	

7.	Communication	Have great meetings with clear objectives, clear preparation, and an aligned agenda; be ready for the tough questions; and become proficient in the strategic asset of *Presentation Mastery*™	
8.	Being Ready	Have a mindset that says, *I will always prep and be ready ahead of time*; be consistently organized; have backup for everything; plan for what-ifs; be presentation ready; and know your risk factor.	
9.	Investing for Your Future	Get advice that will help you uncover your *Blind Spots*. Strategically build your personal brand and develop a memorable, influential persona; plant seeds, invest in your future, and reward yourself often.	
10.	Health	Get clear on who you want to become, get good professional advice, and then build your health goals and actions around that vision. Control your diet, get the right exercises, and manage stress.	
11.	Arsenal	Keep an arsenal of tools to give you leverage in presenting your message, executing faster, and adding value. Exceed expectations by planning your arsenal ahead.	
12.	Force Multipliers	Utilize your phone to create leverage and multiply your results. Use Dropbox or an online system to back up your files. Take strategic notes and use checklists to maximize results.	
13.	Habits	Notice patterns and turn them into the right habits. Think like successful people think and do what successful people do. Execute to the point of habit, and strategically move things into the automatic zone. Strategically create foundational habits.	

If there were some areas you still fell below 8 on, I strongly encourage you to review those topics in this book now and get started right away pushing that needle farther up the scale. If you do that, I believe you'll be able to look back a year from now and see a huge impact on your results.

I also encourage you to give copies of this book to the members of your team, friends, and even family members to help them achieve extraordinary results in their lives. I've seen it happen time and again when people come into my private RESULTS studio and the light comes on when they "get" the power of preparation. And I've seen the incredible results that over three decades of strategic preparation have brought to my own life, both personally and professionally. I want that for you, as well, so get started now. There's power in preparation!

ABOUT THE AUTHOR

When many of the world's top achievers seek a strategic expert to help them accelerate their results, they are eventually drawn to Tony Jeary. Tony is the authority on RESULTS and has committed his career to studying and helping others think better and achieve more. If you want to better your life, your career, your organization, and your results, you need to know Tony.

Tony was raised by entrepreneurial parents and grandparents who thrived on identifying and pursuing new opportunities to serve others. His father taught him the powerful principle that has driven Tony's professional and personal life: "Always give more than is expected." Exceeding expectations is the common thread that every Tony Jeary client experiences firsthand. Tony has advised people around the world (in some fifty countries) for over thirty years. He has published more than four dozen books, now in over a dozen languages. And he has worked with CEOs from many of the Fortune 500 companies and entrepreneurial families from the Forbes Richest 400. Tony has been described as a "gifted encourager" who facilitates positive outcomes for others. His list of personal and professional relationships approaches 40,000 people, whom he connects with and nourishes out of his sincere interest and desire for shared success.

Tony's clients include individuals and organizations who are involved globally. He personally coaches the presidents of organizations like Ford, Walmart, Samsung, TGI Fridays, New York Life, Firestone, Sam's Club, and many more.

Tony has personal experience with both success and failure. He made and lost millions before he reached the age of thirty. That early experience with failure propelled him to help others live smart, live on purpose, and be their very best. Today he walks the talk and practices the distinctions that characterize success, both personally and professionally, sharing daily and encouraging others to think strategically about everything. He is blessed with a terrific marriage of over twenty-five years, two great daughters (both of whom he has co-authored books with), and one fantastic son-in-law. Tony currently lives and works on his estate in the Dallas/Fort Worth area where his private RESULTS Studio is located. info@tonyjeary.com

WHAT TONY JEARY INTERNATIONAL CAN DO FOR YOU

RESULTS COACHING

Advice Matters, if it's the right advice. Having coached the world's top CEOs; published hundreds of books, videos, and courses; and advised clients in virtually every industry, across six continents, and at every stage of growth, Tony has positioned himself with a unique track record to take serious high achievers to a whole new level of results. He carefully selects a few clients to coach each year and is devoted to seeing those clients achieve extraordinary success.

INTERACTIVE KEYNOTES

Tony not only energizes, entertains, and educates; he also has his team work strategically and smartly with event teams to make his part as well as the entire experience a super win. An hour with Tony often changes people's lives forever and impacts an organization's results immediately. He delivers high value with a smart fun factor, and he freely shares best practices that both teams and people can really use.

STRATEGIC ACCELERATION FACILITATION PLANNING

Tony can do in a single day what takes many others days and even weeks to accomplish. He gets people to think strategically and has refined a process so powerful that the world travels to his RESULTS compound to experience clarity, focus, and the ability to synergistically execute. He provides at your fingertips three decades of best practices, processes, and tools for accelerating dramatic, sustained results in any organization.

Collaborative Relationships

TJI selectively partners with a handful of select organizations in an annual collaborative arrangement where we pour our knowledge and wisdom into the top leader(s) and their entire organization(s) and help build a super-charged, motivated, and engaged High-Performing Team We align with top entrepreneurs and C-Level management's vision and become an extension of them. The bottom line is, we help: Clarify Vision and Focus on What Matters Most—High Leverage Activities (HLAs)—so people and entire organizations can execute and get the right results faster!

"Change your thinking change your results; it's that simple."
—Tony Jeary
Tonyjeary.com

Join us on the Results Faster! App

We are excited to share with you the Results Faster! app, which is available on the web for all devices. To get started, go to https:// tony-jeary.ihubapp.org and click the Login button in the top right corner. If this is your first time logging in, click on "Register." Once registered, you then have instant access to our Gold Level channels, which include our most popular, most requested resources! Use the left-hand menu to view the channel numbers. Join any channels that are of interest to you, and the content will populate right on the home page of your Results Faster! app.